My Riding Days
Return

Marlitt Wendt

My Riding Days
Return

A guidebook to taking up the reins again

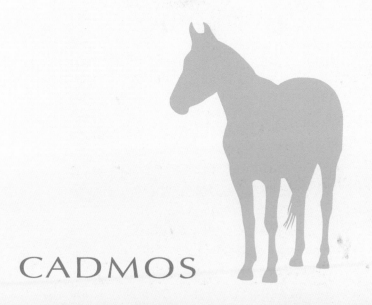

CADMOS

DISCLAIMER

The author and publisher have compiled the contents of this book to the best of their knowledge and in good faith. The author and publisher cannot be held responsible for any injury to human or animal as a result of actions and/or decisions taken based on information contained in the book.

PUBLISHING INFORMATION

Copyright © 2013 by Cadmos Publishing Ltd, Richmond Upon Thames, UK
Copyright of original edition © 2012 by Cadmos Verlag GmbH, Schwarzenbek, Germany
Translation: Chloe Jacquet
Design: Ravenstein + Partner, Verden
Setting: Das Agenturhaus, Munich
Cover photograph: Cornelia Ranz
Content photo: Cornelia Ranz
Unless specified otherwise
Editorial of original edition: Anneke Fröhlich
Editorial of this Edition: Christopher Long
Printed by: Westermann Druck, Zwickau

British Library Cataloguing in Publication Data
A catalogue record of this book is available from the British Library.

Printed in Germany

ISBN 978-0-85788-011-6

Contents

Contents

Foreword: Heaven on Earth ...

... Many of us, as children, sought heaven and found it on a horse's back. Yet at puberty or as young adults our priorities or circumstances often change; many previously horse-mad teenagers push riding and horses to the background.

In the beginning, your relationship, professional training or family commitments take over. But then usually after about ten to fifteen years the memories of the best experiences of your youth and childhood come flooding back. The need to be close to horses resurfaces and financial circumstances often give rise to the dream of owning a horse.

Many, however, who wish to transform the dream of riding into actually putting their foot back in the stirrup, wake up to a harsh reality: neither does the contact with horses meet expectations, nor does that old feeling of happiness really kick in again. On top of that a whole series of fears and uncertainties, which were never felt as a child, come flooding in.

The spontaneity and light-heartedness of childhood seem to have been left behind somewhere. That's how dreams often turn into disaster.

So where does heaven on earth lie? Can we find it again through riding and contact with the horse, that happy memory which we associate with our childhood?

I should like my book to help that comeback really fulfil what we have yearned for with all our heart: to build up an intimate relationship with the horse and experience utter freedom with this animal. Expectations are high, and thus discourage many from making small steps on the road to sheer joy. A childhood dream can become a viable vision of the future on condition that the personalities of both the returning rider and his or her equine partner remain in the foreground.

In order to follow a clear path without having to endure a whole host of training methods, most of which are totally unsuitable for most people, this book focuses on the systematic study of an individual's desires. This includes using suitable techniques taken from psychology, mental training, visualization and practical relaxation methods. In this way the book will accompany the reader on his or her very own journey to personal happiness with the horse.

Marlitt Wendt, February 2012

The author, Marlitt Wendt, with her Haflinger, Chihiro.

The
ðream
of riding

From childhood dream to a vision of the future

A 15-year break from riding cannot simply be brushed away and you cannot just pick up where you left off. Everyone has moved on, your own dreams and goals have perhaps been deferred. The break has had an effect on several levels. Firstly there's the physical aspect: an adult's physical sensations are vastly different from those of a youngster. How well and for how long we used to ride and how much sport was done in the intervening non-riding years will influence whether we can relate more or less to a horse's movements. In addition, our emotional perception of the riding world has changed. The conscious mind shapes our view of the universe and brings out all kinds of fears and thoughts. Re-igniting our childhood and picking up our equestrian past where we left off simply won't work. That is why it makes sense to deal with our own wishes in detail.

Take time to remember your own riding past in detail.

A summary of your personal riding history

Life leaves its mark on each one of us. We are all shaped by our own experiences, our complex web of relationships with our fellow humans, our school education, training or studies, our professional status, our health and many other factors. For many of us, the desire to venture back into the saddle stems from a longing to bring our carefree childhood back to life again, with its light-heartedness and complete lack of obligations and responsibility.

For example, many of those who consider getting back into the saddle get angry with themselves for ever stopping riding. If we hadn't done so, we would not be so uncertain and seemingly incapable now but rather we would be sitting securely in the saddle with an amazing seat and supple movements... . That is of course a little exaggerated, but we can see in this thought pattern that many people, for whatever reason, cannot accept their past decision.

This way of dealing with the past is of limited use for the future. It is not very constructive to blame yourself or to resent your parents who, for example, refused to fund any more riding lessons after your eighteenth birthday. The past only helps you plan for the future when you are at peace with it, when you embrace our own riding history and use it to look ahead.

That was a long, long time ago...

A good exercise to get in touch with your own buried wishes and desires is to record life's most important experiences in chronological order. First, concentrate on all your experiences that had an equestrian theme and then on all the other various areas of life, in order perhaps to reveal some surprising connections.

Place a piece of paper straight in front of you on the table and draw a line from left to right. This timeline symbolizes your life up until now and covers not only your past life with horses but also your later riding-free life. On this line, you can mark approximate points in time representing events which have had an emotional meaning for you. Here you can record actual experiences – good or bad – as well as influential films, books or events.

If you just consider your own individual timeline: what can you identify in those landmarks? Did experiences from other areas of your life have any influence on your time as a rider? When and why did they result in a break? When and why did they contribute to a planned return to the saddle? What are the core themes relating to horses? Did you mainly record competition results and positive feedback from riding teachers? Or do you clearly remember each individual riding school horse you got to know as a child? It is important when creating the timeline to recall emotionally charged events as impartially as possible. Consider yourself to be a historian interested in your own story and only interpret it later when all the events have been compiled.

The past does not determine the future. Just because someone used to compete in show jumping in the past does not mean that they have do the same in their second riding career. If you realize that you now prefer to enjoy the outdoors, then hacking is probably preferable to a dressage lesson in an indoor arena.

Perhaps your dream is to ride again, to explore nature together with a horse and enjoy that closeness riding bareback.

Back in the saddle

To get back in touch with experiences from your youth as smoothly as possible, it is helpful to take stock of your own riding history. What was important to you? How far did you get? What frightened you?

Before you turn to your current knowledge and skill levels, it's important that you face up to your own visions, goals and ideals. Only someone who knows where they want to go will manage to set out on that journey. The image of the herd of horses (see below) should be the link to your own inner wishes. Take some time to observe the picture. Appreciate the mood, the colours, the details. Now comes an important part of the exercise: close your eyes and visualize the image again with your inner eye. Now how do the horses appear? Are they still the same? Where are they going? What happens next? Is there a little movie running through your mind in which you are perhaps involved? Allow that first picture just simply to go by in

When you look at this herd of horses, what springs to mind?
Let your imagination guide you and uncover your desires.

The dream of a close relationship with a horse slumbers within many of us.

your mind and wait for your own images to come to the surface. Which feelings do you associate with your personal pictures? Do they include real memories, thoughts or experiences? How far back do they go?

Now if I ask you what horses symbolize to you, it becomes useful to note down the answers in detail, since horses and our relationship with them mean totally different things to different people. While one person immediately associates the symbol with freedom and can see many mental images of galloping herds of horses, someone else might think of the key word "harmony" and see mainly horse and rider embodying a strong connection and relationship. These pictures certainly mirror a part of our subconscious desires.

In addition to those associations we have mentioned, returning riders most frequently describe ideals of strength, often represented by a powerful rearing or galloping stallion in all his beauty, of joy in movement and elegance, or else of mares with foals representing motherhood, love and care. There are also visions of concrete situations, for example the dream of winning a competition or images of moments of farewell. Also common are dreadful visions of bolting or rearing horses or those exhibiting their natural primal force which we face helplessly and in fear.

Only we can decipher the pictures which appear in our own dreams and associate feelings with them. This association is all the more helpful because it makes it clearer why, after so many years, we start to think again about returning to the horse. These pictures are almost a snapshot of our subconscious and clarify our dreams and longings but also our worries and fears. They can, to a certain extent, become guides and help us in our reorientation towards a future with horses.

The pictures also often reveal the inner ambivalence we feel towards the horse: while on the one hand we dream of the feeling of freedom galloping on a strong stallion along the beach, wanting to share his strength and speed and experience nature above the beat of his hooves, the sound of the sea and the spray of the water, there is, on the other hand, the horrible scenario of a failed jump and the resulting fall and injury. We find ourselves on an emotional rollercoaster. Horse visions show us both our dreams, which are important for our satisfaction and happiness, but also our worst fears which we have to confront. The dreamy images are as varied as the horror scenarios. Based on these different visions, the return to the saddle will be experienced on different levels for each and every one of us.

"I always get everything wrong"

In order to progress from an equestrian point of view, it is crucial to examine your own handling of criticism. No one in the process of learning can avoid receiving criticism from riding teachers and other riding school pupils. If we allow ourselves to be disheartened too much by this, then soon all we'll be able to see is what we cannot do. Learning to ride is a life mission for everyone. It is so complex that no one, not even the most famous international competitive riders, will ever reach perfection.

It is therefore healthiest to immediately let go of your aim for perfection. It will be far more realistic to decide to give your very best and learn things gradually. If you receive outside criticism, it is first of all important not to take it as a personal attack, but to embrace it non-judgementally and verify its truth. Don't take it personally: every riding school has its own gang of know-it-alls and they should not be given the least opportunity to influence your own personal path negatively. There will always be those who prefer to sit in the tackroom criticizing others rather than working on their own mistakes.

Let us stick to our own path and follow it at our own pace. Every lifelong learning path is as individual and unique as the human and horse that tread it together.

Visions – of Pegasus, unicorns and centaurs

Many of our visions cannot even be found in reality but rather originate from a fantasy

world. They are symbols of desires slumbering deep within us. When, as children, we wanted to experience boundless freedom with Pegasus, the winged horse, or merge with a magical horse to become a centaur, or when we were touched by the gentle purity of the unicorn, that is when we were looking for equivalents in reality.

These dreamed of, and often subconscious, visions are a powerful motivation for anyone wanting to get back in the saddle. In our minds we associate the horse with that apparently wholesome time of our childhood before the world began to get more complicated and confusing. As adults, we can now allow ourselves to retrieve a piece of that happy time, since we sometimes need half a lifetime before finding out at last what our heart's desire really is.

If even small details link together into a meaningful chain and you start remembering the smell of a horse, the sound of its teeth grinding as it nibbles its hay and its soft, friendly nose, then it's about time you dared take the first step towards that equestrian dream. If you can feel that deep desire then you will succeed in incorporating this wonderful hobby into your daily life. Each person will choose a different method to free up the time. Perhaps there are domestic chores which your partner can take over. In any case the role of "family manager" can certainly be cut back just for once.

Face up to the challenge and your dreams. Maybe you will not be able to ride every horse, but you can learn something from each one of them and about yourself and your relationship with these fascinating creatures.

Horses trigger deep emotions in every one of us and we delight in their beauty and power.

Developing your own aims and objectives

At the beginning of any goal is a thought, a mental image of what could be and not just of what is. If we look at the things we can do well, then we should think of broadening and adding to these skills. Be kind to yourself – don't just focus on your weaknesses as you've certainly analysed those more than enough, but also your strengths. Let's compare it to planning a holiday. First you start by choosing a destination. Often you will have a vision, perhaps of the beach and the sea, and then you put it into a specific context, possibly in a relaxed atmosphere which you associate with the Caribbean. It's only then that you start getting active and try to turn a pleasant dream into a reality.

This is just the sort of methodical process that you can use for your return to an equestrian life. Let us imagine exactly what we want. Obviously we probably aren't going to become top-level, all-round riders at age 75. But that dream of adventure with a

There are many ways of practising our freshly rediscovered hobby.
The sporting aspect does not have to be at the forefront.

horse in the great outdoors can just as well be fulfilled with gentle hacks together. So you must adapt your desires to reality. Which skills would you specifically like to develop or discover? Is it something that you already did as a child and want to relive, such as riding out bareback on a pony in the sunshine? Or do you dream of new challenges? Have you always wanted to ride at a tölt or learn the art of dressage from an old Master? If the goal is clear then a concrete plan can be developed. In this way the individual stages on the path to a successful return to the saddle can be defined and tackled one by one, step by step.

The dream of owning your own horse

Of course for many people, going back to riding on school horses or a shared horse after a long break is only one step. In the long term there is also that long-held desire for your own horse, an animal for which you are responsible, in which you can confide and with which you can progress together.

This step should be considered very carefully as this new family member would not only cost a lot of time and money, but if well looked after can live until it is 30 and will require a lot of care and devotion. Older people wanting to get back in the saddle should consider the future of their horses carefully in case the horse should outlive them. One good way of testing your responsibility within a defined framework might be to try taking a share in a horse.

A realistic appreciation of your own riding ability is important when considering acquiring your own horse. All too often we find retired racehorses in the hands of well-meaning riders who want to help an animal but who are then unfortunately totally overwhelmed by the task. The extreme sensitivity of a thoroughbred, perhaps combined with bad memories of the racetrack, is not for a beginner who, up till now, has merely ridden a few comfortable circles on a lunge rein.

Young horses and foals are generally not for returning riders, however cute and cheap they are. Their training requires endless patience and, above all, expertise. A lack of these will make neither horse nor owner happy.

The horse must therefore match the abilities and needs of its human. The saying goes: the more inexperienced the rider, the more experienced the horse should be. Even though the fate of a so-called "problem horse" is touching, such a horse belongs in professional hands and is in no way a suitable leisure partner for a returning rider who simply wants to spend a few pleasurable hours outdoors with his or her horse.

The "right horse" does not exist – each one is special in its own way just as each person must follow his or her own personal path towards that horse. The perfect "back-to-riding" horse will help you find inner equilibrium. It reacts calmly without being boring, it is confident when you need a strong partner and will delight you with its sound training from which you can benefit, and gives you the affection you crave.

Learning
to ride using all your senses –
Mastering the comeback

During your schooldays you will have come to understand that each person learns in a different way. What seems easy to one person can remain totally incomprehensible to another. When it comes to riding, there are many learning styles. As the old saying goes, you can only learn riding by riding, but for each of us, the ways and means in which that learning is constructed, and the freedom to experiment, are fundamental. For both human and horse, motivation and inner preparation are essential for learning success. We will more often pursue those things that we enjoy and therefore become even more successful at them, rather than those things for which we feel less enthusiasm. As a returning rider you are most probably already motivated by both your objectives and your happy memories of those beautiful times spent around horses.

When it comes to the learning process, each individual has a preference for different input channels. Some assimilate information best through dialogue, others will prefer remembering associations they have tested for themselves.

How does the human being learn?

Motivation alone is not enough. An essential component of successful learning is the opportunity actively to shape the whole learning process. It could get unpleasant quite quickly if your personal learning style does not match the chosen training method and type of lessons.

Of course we have to learn. But we all differ in the way in which we absorb and process information. Each of us learns via different input channels. The primary channels are the visual channel (absorbing learning information through our eyes), the auditory channel (hearing), the cognitive channel (understanding), and the haptic channel (touch). We also learn by association – things we have seen and recognized, things we have heard and been shown, theories we have understood and personal experiences acquired throughout our lives.

Using all this information, our brains build a picture which helps us learn to master our lessons. Which channel is most important varies from person to person as well as from lesson to lesson. Often we receive insufficient guidance when learning in riding lessons. We are expected to get a feel for the horse and the aids just by repetition alone. What is more, we are often just given abstract teaching phrases such as "keep contact with our seat". How that should actually happen in practice remains a riding instructor's secret.

Whereas some riding school pupils find it sufficient that the riding instructor talks to them, most would also like an illustrated explanation and theoretical background information in order to comprehend the riding techniques. They will learn particularly well if they are shown pictures or videos where riders can be seen executing a lesson correctly. They can then run these images again and again in their mind's eye. Even advanced riding school pupils can take on the function of role model.

The individual experience of schooling exercises is indeed too short in many riding lessons. Every rider can get to know his or her body better through seat and balance exercises. A well-trained school horse can help a pupil to experience complex schooling exercises such as their first lateral movements and to feel in harmony with the horse.

How does the horse learn?

Horses learn from the consequences of their own behaviour. If a certain behaviour is rewarded, then the horse will exhibit it more often; if it is not rewarded or even leads to an unpleasant feeling, then the horse will exhibit this particular behaviour less often in future. Learning happens constantly – it cannot just be absorbed from one riding lesson. Riding school horses draw their own conclusions from the behaviour of their riding pupils and riding instructors. Depending on the philosophy behind the riding method being taught, a horse will have greater or fewer pleasant experiences which will have a strong effect on its psyche and well-being.

It is important to think about how school horses have been trained in any particular riding establishment. Every riding instructor should explain the basis of their training system and associated philosophy of life to their students. If, however, we prefer a different training philosophy or way of behaving around horses from that of our trainer's, then we are likely rapidly to run into moral conflict.

Even now, for example, most horses are trained using the pressure–release system. This means that the horse is given a stimulus, perhaps a riding aid, lightly at first, which is then stopped as soon as the horse reacts in the way it is expected to. If the horse fails to react, then the pressure is gradually increased till the horse finally reacts and yields to the pressure. Anyone learning to ride according to this principle will reach the point where the riding instructor will instruct them to increase that pressure. If, for ethical reasons, we do not want to increase the pressure, then we will not find any alternatives within this particular system.

Horses can become accustomed to unusual objects without any stress
if they are given plenty of praise during the training process.

This then means applying alternative styles of training and riding systems in which the focus is on reward, such as, for example, clicker training (see also page 27). This means rewarding the horse each time it does something right. In this way the horse will be strongly motivated to work for people. Rewards can take the form of treats, or, depending on what is asked of the horse, can also be intensive stroking, a friendly word, an enthusiastic reaction to the horse's success or a game played with the horse.

Training philosophies, which are the building blocks of any particular training method, can basically be distinguished by their approach to the horse's psyche. Each of us must bear in mind the tangible aims for our riding life as well as the path which leads to it. If we don't, the dream will just burst like a soap bubble.

When looking for a possible riding school, many of us think first of all about a future riding style. In other words you think right now about a distant objective in its concrete form. It makes a difference whether your dream is of a Western-style trail horse, a rustic Icelandic horse or an elegant baroque horse. The objective determines the path, because when you consider the fully trained horse, you have an image of the specific support, requisite basic skills and equipment that you will require. When you are setting objectives, riding styles differ considerably one from the other, as do the paths that lead there. Even the rider's seat, how the reins are held and the aids applied vary from one riding style to another depending on which training objective is to be attained. Emphasis will be placed on different points at different times depending on these training objectives. While many dressage horses are rarely or never trained across country but are taught to be collected from an early age,

some Icelandic horse trainers teach their horses out in the country right from the beginning, accompanied by experienced horses, and only ride them in the school to correct faults or train them in special paces.

The basic aims of a horse's training should, in fact, be identical for all styles of riding. What we want is a positive horse working cooperatively with us that is ridden in an anatomically correct manner within the limits of its physical capabilities, one that has been schooled, that knows the aids and is, if possible, uncomplicated and calm. The riding style then determines what else needs to be learnt, how the aids are applied and the choice of equipment.

As far as the horse's psyche and our own assessment of the philosophy are concerned, the actual content of the training is of lesser importance. What is far more important is the training method itself, in other words the way in which the horse is trained. When learning, we as riding pupils need to reconnect with our basic beliefs. Only when we can empathize with how the horse should be handled, how it is trained, how it is treated in moments of stress or alleged mistakes, can we be in a position to decide whether we really want to learn those particular means and techniques.

The various methodologies can be explained and divided into different categories by looking at the learning behaviour of the horse. Horses learn things, commands or aids by associating the trainer's behaviour within the training situation and external circumstances with their own experiences and emotions. They remember a new experience or aid as being positive if they felt comfortable during that particular situation or negative if they felt uncomfortable. As we have already stated, horses more often do those things

Little games or even running together can be motivating for the horse.

which have been rewarded in whatever shape or form, and refrain from behaviour which has not been rewarded.

The different training methods can be divided into two broad approaches: one training technique exerts pressure on the horse to prompt a reaction or a movement. This is then channelled in the desired direction and guarantees the horse peace and a break as soon it follows the trainer's wishes. This training method is the widely used Pressure–Release System. The other principal training method motivates the horse to show desired behaviour more frequently by using reward.

A quick look at how a school horse is trained

In order to clarify the various procedures involved in training a school horse, let's take a quick look at the common lungeing or free schooling of the horse. According to the traditional training guidelines of the FN (the German governing body for equestrian sports), the horse is lunged on a circle. The direction in which it moves is determined by the position of the person holding the lunge, the pressure which the latter exerts with their body language and the lungeing whip and also the length of the lunge rein. The horse also learns to accept to go at the right pace and in the right direction through the propulsive pressure of the aids.

The fundamental principles of the "alternative" methods work in a similar way. These training systems, more established in Western riding, include the Horsemanship Methods, Parelli training or Monty Roberts' Join-Up method. Here the horse is not moved on with a lunge and lunge whip but through reinforced, menacing human body language and movements and a build-up of pressure using rope, lasso or whip. In both these methods, when the pressure ceases, the horse gets the message that it has behaved in the way the trainer wanted. From a pedagogical and psychological point of view, these pauses in pressure aren't really the true rewards that these trainers often maintain they are, but are merely a cessation of previously built-up pressure. By definition a real reward is adding something which is pleasurable to the horse without having previously built up the pressure; this principle does not exist here.

Work with rewards is found in the opposite training method, known as positive reinforcement. In this approach, every time the horse assumes a correct position as required by the trainer, it gets a reward. In order to make this process easier, many positive horse trainers use a so-called target, for example a pointer stick, to orient the position and determine the speed at which the horse should move. The stick indicates to the horse that it will get a reward if it finds itself with its head level with the marker at the desired speed and distance it has been taught. Rewards are given according to what the horse likes. Depending on preference and the aim of the exercise, this can be stroking, vocal praise or even a treat. During the training phase the horse will get plenty of rewards, which means that there are many interruptions in the movement flow. However, little by little the time periods in which a horse circles round on the lunge increase. The best known form of reward training is clicker training, in which the horse is conditioned to respond to the sound of a clicker during a conditioning phase. At first the horse learns to expect a treat after every click, and that the click and treat are given each time it acts in the way the human expects. The advantages of clicker training are that it is an extremely effective, precise form of reward, it has a non-violent approach and is a training method which is based on the horse's cognitive ability.

It's not just a question of riding

When a returning rider assesses a possible riding establishment, the establishment's training principles are a deciding factor. Is the training aimed at rapid "success", in other words preferably on an easy horse that has no ideas of its own, or should the training encourage the development of the horse's personality as well as being of use to us humans?

The consequences of excessive human ambition are manifold and range from undue physical demands on the horse to chronic stress. Many horses that are pushed to do too much too soon often end up not being able to do anything correctly. They suffer from lack of concentration, are stressed and, depending on their nature, become restless or phlegmatic.

Understanding and long-lasting education can only work if you adapt to the learning speed of each individual horse, give it the opportunity to cooperate and understand, give it those all-important breaks, and reinforce what has been learnt through repetition. In general, those who have given the horse all the time it needs will reach their objective the fastest. The general atmosphere during the training process is paramount; a positive feeling when learning promotes sustainability.

Fundamentally, variety in the school horse's daily life is extremely important. Horses are by nature curious and get bored if exercises are always carried out in exactly the same way. Having said that, there is a very fine line here from mental overload since many horses also require a certain routine. During the training of an all-round school horse, it should be decided which aspects are to be learned and in which order. Simply going out of the indoor school and into the countryside can offer some variety. A horse shouldn't immediately be trained to become an elegant dressage horse, a safe driving horse and a performing circus horse all at the same time. That would be far too much, and a riding pupil would only feel totally confused on such a horse.

Usually horses like to work together with other horses. A walk with other horses or a peaceful group hack in the surrounding area offers both a change and a release of tension. In addition, many horses love more playful activities. A game of horse football could occasionally be included in a riding lesson, or some easy TREC obstacles tried out. These strengthen mutual trust, afford change and promote communication between horse and human.

The FN's training scale provides a very good overview of the essential learning stages that can be achieved, depending on the philosophy of the different training methods. Schooling exercises, both in-hand and ridden, originate from classical dressage and give the horse's body greater flexibility and power. A good physical feeling can be reinforced through Tellington Touch Training. In particular, Western riders' trail obstacles and their own particular riding style can fulfil the everyday, relaxing needs of the leisure rider.

In conclusion, a school horse's training is best approached from many sides once we have decided on a particular training

philosophy. In this way, both we and our horse's learning environment will become totally reliable. The horse knows its boundaries and understands what we are trying to get it to do. Above all, this requires a decision to be made and followed through. You are the one who has to decide, according to your moral ideals, how you want to see a school horse being handled under the supervision of a trainer, and at what price your learning objectives should be met. Have you decided "how"? Thanks to your decision you can follow

your own chosen direction and in line with the skills of your preferred type of horse. Training should be pleasurable for both sides and bring feelings of success.

As returning riders, we are not only responsible for our own actions but we also constantly have to make important decisions which, hopefully, take the well-being of the school horse into account. Humans are always being influenced by their desires, unknown fears and the expectations of those around them. When we finally face the de-

Circus tricks and games provide welcome variety for horse and human and foster the relationship between them.

cision of which riding school to choose for our first riding lesson and decide which training philosophy to go for, we are confronted with a mountain of external pressure.

For example, how will riding friends of ours who have made a different decision react?

Anybody who wants anything to do with horses in whatever shape or form has to make that crucial decision of which path to set off on. Good, horse-friendly riding is not a question of riding style but of the underlying training philosophy.

Good balance helps the rider to relate to the horse's movements and to master the first dressage lessons.

Anyone prepared to work on themselves and their seat will be rewarded with a relaxed horse.

Motor learning

We need to access our subconscious if we really want to learn to ride again. Children learn intuitively. This is why as children we preferred doing things without the need for lengthy explanations. For example, let's think back to bicycle riding. When you learned this highly complex exercise, you certainly didn't pay any attention to your parents' lectures about how to brake or the correct way to cycle round a bend. You just got on and rode your bike. Of course you had a few falls, but your body adapted its movements to the bicycle's requirements.

The saying goes: whoever wants to ride the waves shouldn't try to change the sea. The same goes for riding. An adult tends to over-analyse. We don't want to look stupid, and would rather skip the beginner stages and know everything immediately. Yet the so-called basal learning experiences such as the intuitive experience of the rocking movement of a horse's back, your own body rotation as the horse turns, or the different perspective from the back of a large animal that you automatically had as a child are extremely important. Constant armchair reasoning will lead to failure. You should certainly take the time to appreciate a horse's movements in their entirety. The following chapters give an outline of the various possibilities for developing your own sense of movement.

Riding
isn't just about riding –
Riding schools and what they offer

A quick look inside any leisure-oriented equestrian magazine immediately reveals the myriad possibilities for enjoying riding as a hobby. Middle-aged women are seen riding on Western saddles, setting off on challenging long-distance rides or enjoying nature on a relaxing hack. Alongside these illustrations are pictures of places where you can pursue your hobby. From glass-fronted modern riding schools to a simple sand outdoor school to an oval tölt track – everything's there, it's just a matter of taste. However, for returning riders, it is extremely important to get to grips with the reality of what is on offer. It will take a mixture of conscious decision and gut feeling to choose the right "how" and "where" for our return to the saddle. The riding establishment closest to home isn't always the best solution for our personal happiness.

Does the atmosphere at the riding school make you want to spend time there?

The choice of a riding school

Before actually going in person to see the riding establishment you are considering, why not first gather a few details on the Internet, in brochures or by telephone? Many riding schools openly share their priorities and philosophy or sporting ambitions. You

would be well advised to consider whether you should really choose a riding school simply because it happens to be convenient-ly located on the way home from work. Stables with young riders and teenagers are often not suitable for more mature re-turning riders. If there is nothing on offer for adults and particularly for returning

A spacious, well-kept outdoor school is ideal for riding lessons.

riders, then you will certainly find yourself surrounded by teenagers during lessons and horse care. The topics of discussion, the possible noise levels and also the teaching style aimed at such groups do not suit everyone. It is therefore worth looking for an establishment that specializes in adults, beginner riders and perhaps even returning riders.

There are various organizations for equestrian sports, including dressage. Affiliation to one or other of these doesn't say everything about a riding school. Affiliations such as these can however help you to assess the focus and quality of the establishment. A riding school has to fulfil certain criteria in order to be recognized as an approved business or association.

There are also, without question, many good businesses offering excellent teaching without such an affiliation. It could be that perhaps the owner simply doesn't see any advantage in going through all the bureaucracy. When in doubt you should always form your own opinion, trust in your gut feeling and never blindly rely on official seals of approval.

The whole atmosphere of a riding school is important for a returning rider. You will only be able to get back to your past

Anyone wanting to explore a specialized discipline such as show jumping needs a jumping arena tailored specifically to the needs of the returning show jumper as well as a reliable schoolmaster.

riding career if you find yourself in an inspiring environment that makes you feel comfortable and encourages you to spend time there. Even the first minutes in a riding establishment can say a lot about whether this is the right place to make your dreams come true. Only in the right place can a second riding life be possible. Take some time to observe the horses, get a feel for the establishment and talk to the directors, staff and riding pupils. Your intuition will let you know whether you could pursue your future hobby here.

Now having decided to resuscitate your riding, it would certainly be helpful to be able to practise all year round and in all weathers. An indoor school or all-weather school is essential for this. A classroom or lounge is also useful for theory lessons. The facilities of each establishment should also be considered in detail. Are there TREC obstacles, mounted games equipment, a safe riding track around the fields? Such an establishment would offer many possibilities for returning to the saddle. If in the long term you envisage learning a specialized discipline, then the necessary facilities need to be available. This could be a well-equipped show jumping arena or a school with a surface specifically for Western reining. A classroom with specialized books, teaching materials, DVD player and projector would make it possible to discuss and deepen the acquired theoretical knowledge.

You may have to compromise on some criteria as there may not be a riding school in your area that can fulfil all your wishes. It can be helpful to make a list of your priorities. This will help you identify those things you simply cannot do without and those that could initially take a back seat. That way it would still be possible to switch to that Western yard with the perfect reining arena and start a competitive career after you have mastered the basics and got back into the old routine.

The school horses: the heart of the riding school

The school horses are the most important "employees" of a riding school. You can learn a lot about the manager's attitude from the quality of their care and how they are handled. Does the manager consider them to be fellow creatures that have feelings, or merely commodities? All horses, and particularly riding school horses that have to accept the burden of ever-changing riders, have the right to a life appropriate to the species and as close to nature as possible.

The further removed the school horse's living conditions are from nature, the less likely the returning rider will be able to learn about the horse and the more likely in the long term that the school horse will suffer from the consequences of inadequate conditions. While until recently it was still common practice to keep horses exclusively in stables, it should nowadays be standard to ensure appropriate and healthy accommodation in so-called open stabling or stabling allowing freedom of movement with generous paddocks and fields and above all in a group with other horses. Each horse also needs appropriate equipment which has been tailored to its needs. Ideally each horse should have its own saddle, bridle and grooming kit.

School horses should be well behaved, friendly and steady enough to carry their pupils. A horse can only do this if it is ridden and cared for in an appropriate manner and above all if it has had versatile training. Training a horse and correcting its mistakes should not be done by the riding

Modern, open stabling is the perfect living environment for horses.

pupils, but should always be done by a professional.

Caring for, equipping and training a horse is extremely expensive. What is more, any horse can fall ill and not be able to be ridden every day. That is why a good riding lesson on a happy school horse is worth its weight in gold. Quality doesn't come cheap. If, as a returning rider, you already have some experience, then the riding school will need to be able to offer you different horses for different lessons. You will appreciate horses with smooth, comfortable paces when doing exercises to

While one rider might prefer to ride a proud Andalusian horse,
another may prefer a more manageable Icelandic horse.

improve your seat, calm hacking specialists for your first rides out, and schoolmasters who will make advanced lessons easier.

In terms of temperament, horses should also be suited to the different needs of the riding pupil. Regaining confidence in your own skills and acquiring a feel for the correct aids is easiest when mounted on a quiet, patient horse. On the other hand more sensitive and reactive horses are better suited for developing the subtleties of riding. We can also explore our physical sensations, which have altered since our youth, by trying out horses of different sizes and builds. Not everyone feels at home on the back of an imposing Friesian, and

A suitable living environment for horses allows our four-legged friends to have close bonds with other horses.

whereas for some a large framed warmblood sport horse might be too powerful, for others, riding a pony would feel like sitting on a rocking horse.

Even if you are not quite one hundred percent familiar with the behaviour of animals and what they are capable of doing, you can still get a feel for their emotional state. Look at the riding school horses straight in the face, in their eyes. What do you see? Do the horses have soft, shining, radiant eyes? Do they seem interested in what's going on, do they notice the people and are they curious about them? Do they exude happiness: do they shine from the inside out? Or do they appear absent: is their expression empty and apathetic? We are hardly likely to find heaven on earth where the animals live in a bleak environment. Happiness cannot be found on top of another creature's back, but rather together with it. If a riding school's horses do not make a good impression, then we humans won't be able to spend carefree leisure time there and should not endorse such an establishment.

The riding instructor: a good teacher

The first duty of an instructor is to impart his or her knowledge to us. To do this, they need specialized knowledge, but also to be in a position to present it in such a way that we can understand it. Pedagogic skill and the ability to instill a harmonious atmosphere and tune into clients' fears and worries cannot be displayed on a trainer's certificate.

For a return to the saddle to succeed, it is absolutely indispensable that the pupil's motivations should match those of the instructor. We have already seen that a return to the saddle is dependent on the fact that we have made it clear to ourselves why we even want to start riding

A good riding instructor always bears the individual needs of his or her pupils in mind.

again and what our personal objective is. In that very same way, the riding instructor also has their own vision, whether conscious or subconscious, as to what they can achieve with their teaching and what they would like to transmit to their students.

There are those ambitious riding instructors who would like to prepare their students for competitions, just as there are those trainers who see the horse as a reliable partner in the great outdoors and would like to provide their pupils with a more emotional approach to such a living creature. Then there are the riding masters who see riding as an art form and would like to convey its cultural and historic aspects. If one tries to impose their motives on the other, then they will end up literally talking over one another.

A lesson cannot succeed if we are expected to grapple with a perfect shoulder-in and its biomechanical details, when what we really need is to gain confidence and get to know the horse. Therefore it is key for returning riders not only to recognize their own motivations, but also to ask the riding instructor about theirs. Alternatively, they can draw their own conclusions as to what they are from what the instructor asserts or from the establishment's presentation. If a marketing brochure shows a picture of a riding instructor whose clothing and equipment embody a model of tradition and history, then you can assume that tradition plays an important role there. If the brochure alludes to breeds and horse pedigrees then you are unlikely to feel at home if you are uninterested in breeding and bloodlines. It also makes a great difference

if the website shows a smiling riding instructor sitting on a Haflinger out in the countryside, or deep in concentration in an arena executing a piaffe on an Andalusian horse.

For some riding instructors, it is accomplishment and skill in all their finer details that are important whilst for others it is togetherness that counts. If your motivations are not in line with those of your riding instructor, you will quickly feel out of place. Relationships with the horse are highly subjective – none is more correct than the other – yet it is vital for riding instructor and returning rider to share their vision in a broadly consistent way.

Beyond the importance of a shared vision of riding, an excellent relationship between instructor and pupil is indispensable. The chemistry simply has to work if we are to feel good in the instructor's care.

The other riding school pupils and you

At the stables you will inevitably come into contact with all sorts of other people who share the same hobby as you, and whose approach to the horse may differ more or less from yours. In a best case scenario you will meet future friends with similar likes and dislikes. If in particular you meet other like-minded returning riders, you will be able to find shared solutions for those particular concerns that emanate from a break in riding and complex family and work commitments. A good stable community leads not only to a relaxed working atmosphere but can also lead to emotional support outside of riding.

It's great when you can develop friendships with like-minded people.

Your personal checklist for choosing a riding school

In order to evaluate and shortlist riding schools that you are considering, it is helpful to draw up an individually tailored list of questions. Here are a few questions you might ask of an establishment:

- Do the school horses live in generous open stables with access to paddocks and fields?
- Are they lovingly cared for, groomed and treated?
- Do they look healthy and well fed? Do they have equipment that is suitable and well looked after?
- Have they been well trained and ridden to correct any further faults?
- Are there plenty of facilities?
- What qualifications does the riding instructor have? Different qualifications will be important depending on each rider's preferences. A coaching certificate may be sufficient for some people but, for others, competition and show success will be important.
- Does the riding instructor have the same motivations as you?
- Do they have your preferred breed of horse?
- Which riding styles are on offer?
- Are the lessons sufficiently varied and is it possible to have theory lessons or specialized courses?

Do the school horses and their equipment look as if they are well cared for?

Each riding style has its own appeal.

Everyone's got talent – but for what?

It isn't always easy to figure out exactly what it is you want. There are innumerable ways to be with horses. Nowadays you can almost get lost in that giant labyrinth of equestrian hobbies. Only 25 years ago things were quite different. As children most of us learned to ride in a typical riding school. Emphasis was placed on a varied grounding in show jumping, dressage and cross-country, whereas groundwork, playing with or desensitizing a horse were unheard of.

Each of us intuitively prefers a particular style of riding. It embodies a particular lifestyle, a special relationship with the horse and differentiates itself in its focus and objectives. Not every rider feels comfortable in every saddle.

Discovering your own talent has a lot to do with the search for inner motivations and desires. Your reasons for getting back in the saddle also depend on your reasons for taking a break. Anyone who couldn't achieve what they wanted at that time, for example who didn't experience that really relaxed feeling riding outdoors, will probably seek that missing element.

We will be good at things we can empathize with, from which we get an emotional connection and a comfortable feeling. This is why we need an honest evaluation of the situation, of how good our riding knowledge used to be or still is, of what we know about the riding style we are aiming for and of our mobility and physical sensations.

I would now like to present the best known and most common types of riding and their objectives, in order to help the returning rider reach a decision.

German equestrian training

In Germany, the current riding guidelines were established about 100 years ago based on military tradition. These were used as a basis for developing the "Richtlinien für Reiten und Fahren" ("Guidelines for riding and driving"). The objective stemming from this tradition is to train a versatile horse that can carry its rider safely cross-country, as well as in the dressage and show jumping arenas. This riding methodology, part of the Skala der Ausbildung ("training scale"), is based on a foundation of dressage

A modern Warmblood with its ample stride is perfect for competitive dressage and show jumping.

training, and promotes the successful combination of rhythm, suppleness, contact with the bit, impulsion, rectitude and collection. The objectives of this riding style can be seen in competitions and are demonstrated in the various disciplines at the Olympic Games.

Returning riders with sporting ambitions will find this type of riding best suited to them. Disciplines such as dressage, show jumping and eventing are those which lead to the greatest physical fitness and agility. The attractive, energetic paces of modern Warmblood horse breeds require a supple seat in the saddle. The tack is usually of a traditional, practical type.

Justifiably criticized in recent years is the rejection of the original precept of a healthy riding horse in favour of ever faster sporting success. Unfortunately nowadays harmony and lightness are often hard to find. Pressure and a whole array of tools are used to accelerate competitive success. Although these are extreme excesses of this particular riding style, the returning rider will need to think carefully about whether sporting ambition should be at the forefront of their hobby.

Western riding

For years now, Western riding has presented an alternative school of equitation. In contrast to the traditional style of riding, it features stimulus-type riding where the horse is not continually constrained by riding aids. Following on from the American cowboy tradition, medium-sized horses with smooth, usually very comfortable gaits and posture are ridden one-handed on a loose rein. In Western riding, a light stimulus should be sufficient to execute a specific movement in a balanced way.

For cowboys the horse used to be a working animal. It needed to work reliably and safely, not

Anyone who enjoys agile horses and casual outfits will probably feel at home doing Western riding.

tire, and let its rider sit comfortably in a Western saddle. These origins are precisely why this riding style leads on the one hand to a casual recreational activity, but on the other hand obviously requires absolute obedience from the Western horse which in turn needs extensive schooling. Great emphasis is placed on functionality and less on creativity and opportunities for development of the horse.

Typical Western horse breeds such as Quarter Horses or Paint Horses are of a practical size and are by nature mostly calm and friendly towards people. Western riding offers the interested rider a broad spectrum of disciplines. There's the ever popular Reining, that incredibly fast Western dressage riding, then there are the cattle disciplines such as Cutting or Working Cow Horse, or else disciplines such as Trail which is a test of dexterity or Pleasure which is a test of rideability.

The elegance and aesthetics of Baroque riding inspire many rider.

Baroque riding

Under the heading of Baroque riding, I should like to encompass the multiple riding styles which are becoming increasingly popular. It includes various branches, each with its own focus according to the teachings of the old German, French or Spanish riding masters. True to their historic role models, these trainers see riding as an art form and wish to promote the noble, expressive movements of the horse while covering the least ground. In addition the horses need to be exceptionally collected and have outstanding balance. The horse's tack and the rider's outfit are as opulent as the movements.

This style of riding predominantly uses horse breeds such as Andalusian, Lusitanian or Friesian. Lightweight horses such as the versatile Welsh Cob and many other medium-sized, squarely built horse breeds also lend themselves to this style of riding. Returning riders wishing to get involved in classical riding will need a keen sense of detail and a passion for dressage. Hacking and relaxation are far down on the scale.

Other specialized types of riding

There are a multitude of other styles of riding and specialized disciplines on offer in the various riding establishments.

One very well-known and, for the leisure rider very appealing option, is riding on a horse with a special gait such as tölt or pace and the inherent unique sensations in the saddle. Another possibility is trekking, where you can enjoy nature on horseback, riding at a leisurely pace over wide areas. Long-distance riding is becoming extremely popular as an endurance sport for both horse and rider, but because of the training required, it is very time-consuming and requires great physical fitness.

The American Tellington Method is particularly well known for its groundwork and massage techniques which promote harmonious intimacy between horse and human and general physical well-being. Various training methods such as the Feldenkrais method, the Centred Riding method, or movement training according to Eckart Meyners offer different approaches to nurturing physical sensation when riding. Clicker training is a system of reward-based learning which can be used in many areas of horse training.

The jolt-free movement of the Icelandic horse's tölt is very easy on the back and its dynamics are exhilarating.

How to
proceed –
Which teaching method suits you?

In order to build up on the riding knowledge acquired in your youth, it would make sense first of all to assess it carefully. Did you ride in the truly sporting sense of the word and did you perhaps have some competitive success or did you complete any riding exams? Or did you perhaps spend a week at a coastal location once every three years during the summer holidays so you could spend a couple of pleasant hours each day riding bareback on a pony? The choice of suitable tuition for the returning rider is dependent on how safe and experienced you used to be in the saddle. Once you have assessed your own ability, you can then find a suitable combination from all the teaching methods and media available.

You can concentrate on your seat and on balance exercises when riding a horse which is being led in-hand.

What is the right style of teaching for you?

To ensure long-lasting success for a planned return to riding, it makes sense to choose a combination of different teaching concepts which are adapted to your own ability, prior knowledge and objectives. Each and every style of teaching is valid and has its own advantages and disadvantages.

The best results will be achieved with a combination of different approaches. A classic way to start after a break from riding could be some lessons on the lunge rein in a secure environment. The advantages are obvious: the horse is directed by the riding instructor standing in the centre, and the pupil can concentrate on getting connected with the animal's movements while reviving the old sense of balance without stress.

Even later on this is a good way of improving your seat. In the long term however, it doesn't make sense to keep riding on a lunge rein because the influence of the rider over the horse is missing and independent riding cannot be learned in this way. Also when the horse's pace increases, the centrifugal force strongly pushes the rider outwards which means he or she needs a greater sense of balance than when riding in a straight line.

Private lesson or group lesson?

In most riding establishments the returning rider can choose between private and group riding lessons. Personally, I think that a combination of both types of lesson is highly advantageous. During a private lesson, the returning rider can concentrate wholly on his or her own needs. In addition, the instructor's specific, detailed feedback will create an intensive learning experience. If you particularly want to include a lot of theory during a session, then a private lesson

A carefully assembled group mutually supports its members who motivate each other to individual success.

During private lessons, the riding instructor can concentrate more on the individual needs of his or her pupil.

could be very helpful. On the other hand, a private lesson can be extremely taxing for the pupil since there are hardly any breaks, the riding instructor is constantly watching you and there is no opportunity to try something out unobserved. Since private lessons are extremely work-intensive, the pupil should be sure he or she is fit enough and has sufficient mental capacity.

Group lessons can help reinforce what was learned during a private lesson and also make it possible to practise and refine certain schooling exercises. Each movement requires a lot of repetition until it penetrates the subconscious and becomes automatic. During this period of time you will not continuously progress, so constant feedback from the riding instructor could at times be counterproductive. The atmosphere during a group lesson lends itself more to group exercises such as quadrilles. The pupils are so focused they cannot always concentrate on the theory being explained by the riding instructor.

Since riding is essentially motor learning controlled by the subconscious, the pupil must learn not to impede his or her body by thinking too much about individual aids. Group lessons can help you loosen up. Group dynamics can also help the learning process. A group which has been well constituted mutually supports its members. Returning riders can share common fears and worries, can motivate each other and experience progress together. Many returning riders find it helps their own riding a great deal if they can see other riders as role models and can replicate a given exercise. It is also easier for the instructor if they can point out an exercise that is successfully carried out and which the other riders can then aim to achieve.

Basically, it is a mistake to think that you learn more during private lessons than in group lessons. Through a combination of these types of training, you will learn many different lessons that will be complementary.

In addition to riding lessons

Riding lessons can be complemented with a first hack in the company of others from the riding school. Here the focus is less on the subject of seat and aids, but more on putting into practice what has been learned while in safe surroundings. Team building with your equine partner and the enjoyment of nature can really be reinforced. If togetherness with the horse was in fact the reason for getting back in the saddle, then hacks should be put on the programme at an early stage.

Many establishments specializing in leisure riding offer rides on a lead rein or have fenced-in outdoor areas where you can try out a hack in total safety before venturing out into the great outdoors.

For most returning riders, theory lessons, reading books and watching training films are vitally important to their equestrian success. Many adults want to understand and grasp what they should be doing and why. We often take an overly intellectual approach to learning to ride and want to reinforce our practical experiences with background knowledge. Also, many horse-related subjects can be discovered such as upkeep, feeding or health care, for which there is little time during riding lessons. A positive side-effect of these activities is that the returning rider is almost constantly occupied with equestrian themes and in the process his or her subconscious will instinctively store up important information. When learning, it is helpful to become familiar with the subject on as many levels as possible.

Additional practical experience on a particular topic can be gained during specialized riding courses or advanced seminars. The benefits of these are that a lot of knowledge can be imparted in one go and the returning rider will feel he or she is making progress in a relatively short space of time. Some riding schools for recreational riders offer intensive week-long courses where the returning rider can benefit from a condensed return to the saddle. Subsequent riding lessons can then begin at a higher level.

Advanced lessons and finer points can be worked on intensively during specialized clinics.

A relaxed learning atmosphere builds trust and boosts self-confidence.

Which learning atmosphere?

The atmosphere during a riding lesson is crucial to success. Someone who feels comfortable will learn far more easily and quickly than someone who is stressed, overstretched or afraid. Mostly it is the riding instructor who sets the atmosphere in a lesson. The returning rider should be on the same wavelength as the instructor and should feel noticed and taken into consideration by them.

Whereas in our childhood the riding instructor was almost always a sort of command centre, today's instructor should have more of a coaching role. Returning riders in particular need their instructor to be a trustworthy companion capable of bringing buried riding knowledge back to the surface, someone who knows how to reduce anxiety and can rejoice in progress. A certain pedagogical skill is necessary to be able to do this as there is a fine line between encouraging and overstretching, between conquering fear and increasing it, or between peaceful practice and boredom. It is also a question of taste whether you prefer to be spoken to humorously or purely impersonally. A good riding instructor can assess their returning rider pupil's skills correctly and will succeed in finding connections with childhood learning experiences.

What can you expect from school horses?

A difficult question for returning riders concerns the well-being of the school horses. As a friend of animals, you should avoid establishments where the school horses are exploited and lead a bleak existence. But how to find the best possible riding school for your return to the saddle in terms of the school's attitude to their horses? The best way is to ask the horses themselves and observe how they behave in their various spheres of life.

Take a look at the school horses within their group, in the grooming area and the way they react around riding pupils. The shining coat of a healthy horse will usually be the first thing you notice. Happy horses

have relaxed movements; their ears are pricked and are turned towards anybody, whether riding pupil or instructor, trying to communicate with them. In addition they seek contact with humans and don't hide

in the farthest corner of the yard or at worst, run away when someone approaches.

Even when being ridden, happy school horses clearly show their contentment with their own work when we look them in the face. Their eyes shine; they are actively aware of their surroundings and try to carry out the exercises being asked of them in a quiet manner. In addition, their mouths and nostrils are not wrinkled up and pinched, but relaxed. Their tails swing

Happy horses shine from the inside out and are closer to humans.

quietly in time with their movements, and their muscles are not noticeably tense.

For me, riding lessons which are inline with animal welfare mean that school horses are allowed to live an altogether horse-worthy life, and are looked after just as well as any privately owned horse.

Self-praise usually suffices

Self-motivation is one of the most important tasks for a returning rider – you keep learning to ride your whole life and in the long term you will only ride successfully if you can stay really motivated over a lengthy period of time. To increase your own motivation, it can be useful to get acquainted with the concept of affirmation, of talking to yourself in a positive manner. This type of positive self-talk is a method which helps us "programme" our subconscious so that we can face our return to the saddle in an optimistic way.

First you have to take into consideration that your consciousness cannot differentiate between fact and fiction; it will always assume that what it is told is true. Someone who often says to themselves "but I can't do that", "I'll never learn that" or "everyone else rides better than me" will tend to find getting back in the saddle far more difficult than someone who talks positively to themselves and says things like "I can already ride quite well", "I'm going to do a quiet, relaxed canter in this lesson", or "I trust my school horse".

Your subconscious mind wants to believe everything you whisper to it, whether it

be true or false, positive or negative. It will detect it, record it and lead you to implement it.

Positive self-talk

We are all in a constant dialogue with ourselves and not talking to ourselves even for a short time is impossible. Many of our inner conversations are trivial, such as "I really must phone my mother again" or "I fancy a strawberry ice cream". But as trivial as they may be, unbeknown to us, they often direct our actions and attitudes. Negative self-talk can lead to self-fulfilling prophecies – to misfortunes which we have virtually conjured up by constantly talking about them.

Our subconscious always seems anxious to focus on the crux of our silent communication. If we keep trying to stop bringing these issues up to the surface, our subconscious will focus precisely on the unwanted said issues and in this way the error will persist. It would be far better to concentrate on a constructive image of our objective: "I'm keeping my foot straight in the stirrup". Our subconscious likes to ignore that little word "not". Phrases containing the word "not" are perceived by our minds as if the negation hadn't been present. Affirmation coaches often quote the famous example of the "pink elephants". If you try not to think about pink elephants, then all you'll see in your mind's eye will be pink elephants going by. Telling yourself you do not want to look down will actually weaken your riding ability as you will programme this mistake even deeper into your subconscious. It would be better to express things positively,

A positive attitude influences our subconscious and its positive impact will also be felt by the horse.

towards the direction in which you should be looking: "I'm directing my gaze between the horse's ears".

It makes sense to conduct positive internal dialogues in a concrete manner. You can happily spice up what you are saying and greatly exaggerate how you express yourself. For example, instead of saying "I'm sitting up straight", you could say, "I'm holding myself like a Spanish Flamenco dancer, proud and straight yet supple and elegant". If that image is inherently consistent with what you want and stimulates your fantasies, then it will have the maximum effect. It needs to feel good when you say it out loud – in the car or in the shower. Only then will it trigger your emotions and get you to react. Later on you can arrange your guiding principles into major topics which support your core statement. Then, if you come back to your example, it will be sufficient just to think of Flamenco dancers. Your subconscious will know which qualities you are referring to.

Inner dialogue can stimulate greater self-confidence.

The riding journal

Keeping a riding journal is a good way of recording thoughts and progress. You can write down how your riding lessons, your courses and theory lectures went as well as your impressions and thoughts with respect to the theme of the horse. Sometimes it can be those little things which seemed quite insignificant at the time which later, on re-reading, become the first incentive to solving a problem.

Knowledge derived from books or films and which was relevant or meaningful for the realization of your dream of getting back on the horse can also be written in your riding journal. This sort of writing activity will help you sort through your own ideas and can be an important prop in the learning process. Why not write while sitting in the field with the horses? Then as you write, your gaze will often be drawn to previously unnoticed details.

Writing thoughts down can often shift your focus and your awareness. It helps to call yourself into question and look for ways of improving your actions. We often only realize how much progress we've made when looking back after a certain period of time. Particular memories that have made a real impression can be very motivating for the future.

Exceptional experiences such as a ride through water can inspire us and could be recorded in our riding diary.

Of
horse
and human –
Etiquette for harmonious co-existence

For many returning riders, the idea of a partnership with a horse plays a particularly important role. Horses represent not only the wild, but also the gentle. They have extremely fast reactions but are just as happy lazing around in the sun. Their complex personalities make us want to understand them and be with them. In this way we can not only gain these noble animals' trust and affection, but they can also inspire our own lives. Your return to the saddle will be particularly successful if you are able to get in touch with both your rational and emotional sides. Anyone who perfects their riding skills, understands the mechanisms for training a horse, respects animals' psyches, whilst being aware of their own feelings towards the horse, will be able to fulfil the dreams of horse riding which date back to their youth.

On a par with the horse

Even on first contact with your four-legged partner, you can gain important experience. Horses can feel precisely whether you are being genuine and how comfortable you feel. They feel the difference, the discrepancy, between whether you are desperately trying to loosen up or whether you are actually relaxed and at ease.

They will recognize your friendly attitude radiating through your whole body language and will behave accordingly. They also show us how our emotions influence

A friendship between human and horse based on respect and trust.

their actions and how they are reflected in both our behaviour and posture. Only someone who manages to fulfil the expectations of their equine partner and accepts them with their own individual personality will succeed in doing what so many dream of: the horse will feel valued and will really communicate with you.

Friendship is the greatest social bonding force amongst horses. Horses are sociable, affectionate creatures that build up and nurture long-lasting relationships with others. Similarly, we, as humans, can build a friendship with the horse if we treat it as an equal, penetrate its being, look at the world from its point of view, relate to its feelings and choose to go down a common path. To attain this, it helps to work on your own presence. When you are with the horse, focus only on him and communicate with him rather than being on the phone or mentally going through your shopping list at the same time. Horses are finely tuned to the attention and concentration of other living beings. Only if you are concentrated on your exercises and keep your own objectives with the horse firmly in mind, will you manage, for example, to get the horse to follow you willingly. A horse is far more likely to be attracted to your relaxed, carefree movements than if you are bored and your boredom is reflected as you shuffle along.

Try an interested and friendly approach when meeting a horse for the first time. Anyone who frightens his or her school horse by marching directly towards it in the field and glaring at it will find that the horse holds back later on during their work together. It makes more sense to make a long slow curve when approaching the horse, to slow down when at a certain distance from its side, or even stand still when approaching a more nervous horse and call it by name.

If it lifts its head and turns towards you, then you can go up to the horse and make direct contact with it. At the same time, observe its body language and facial expression so you can anticipate any potentially hostile behaviour. If the horse approaches you with friendly, pricked ears and a soft mouth, then you can step up your contact, perhaps by stretching out your hand for it to sniff, or scratching it on the withers. Only begin your training session together once you have greeted one another politely.

Two beings – one direction

Closeness with a horse is particularly enjoyable when you are both looking in the same direction and following the same path. This is where your intuition and sensitive, cognitive ability will help you make contact with the horse and feel whether it is really following you willingly or whether it is holding back out of fear. You will perceive changes in the horse's posture, its stiffening muscles or changes in breathing for example and, based on previous experience, your body will react intuitively with fear or confidence. To be able to handle horses in a relaxed manner, it can be helpful to get come to grips with your role of leader. Being a leader does not mean forcing the horse to go anywhere. Rather the word denotes an ability to focus and concentrate on your self-imposed objective so that the horse can recognize and accept it too.

As an exercise, when leading your horse in-hand, imagine that you are striding towards your goal along a solid line. Walk straight along your imaginary track and follow it without wavering to the left or to the right. Easier said than done. It could be useful therefore to practise following

We follow our path as though on an imaginary line and we do
not allow our attention to be diverted by little distractions.

a line drawn in the sand. You can sharpen
your focus when riding by fixing a point on
the horizon, for example a group of trees
or a building. Now concentrate your attention on that distant point without letting
yourself be distracted by details along the
way.

Our ego often puts stumbling blocks in
the way of gaining leadership qualities.
Each time we do something, not because
it is the correct thing to do in a particular
circumstance but rather because we don't
want to look stupid or because we want to
appear in a better light, our school horse

will feel the discrepancy between appearance and reality, dependent on its temperament, will react either with uncertainty or refusal. This is particularly true of returning riders as they were usually far more advanced when they were younger and now have to admit that they will have to take a few steps back in order to feel comfortable when returning to the saddle.

Using the voice as an aid

The voice can be a valuable aid when riding or handling horses. It can have a stimulating or a calming effect, can instruct the horse to act in a particular way or reward his performance. The voice is often misused in riding stables: horses get yelled at or orders are shouted out. To me, using the voice as an aid in this way shows a lack of respect to the horse. Friendly, polite communication should be the rule. When choosing a stable, the returning rider should take note of the tone of voice used when addressing both human and horse. Our own choice of words always reflects to some extent our attitude towards the animal and our tone of voice betrays our emotions to the sensitive horse.

Trust and feeling

If you want to regain the intuitive behaviour of your childhood towards horses, you should be aware that horses are keen observers. They can perceive the slightest change in posture, facial expression or breathing and they will draw their own conclusions. Neither uncertainties nor overbearing behaviour can be hidden from them. They sense our emotions and trust in people who have a positive, confident presence.

Everything you do has meaning to the horse. It reads your body language constantly. To get an idea of the way you present yourself, you could perhaps have yourself filmed so that you can see for yourself how you appear around horses. Can you recognize your uncertainties or underlying irritability? Which emotions are you expressing? To become more aware of your body, why not try this out: at home, imagine various emotions and find out how you would express them and which movements you would use. How do you express joy? Do you jump up and down or do you move around smoothly? Or what does suppressed anger look like – do you raise your shoulders, tighten your muscles and move awkwardly?

Making contact with the horse provides a good exercise in concentration and also nurtures your feelings towards her. For example, when does the school horse register that you have come to collect her from the field and that you want to make contact with her? Usually it is before you actually talk to her and want to put a halter on. Take a look and by observing the horse's reactions you will see that as soon as you enter the field, the horse knows which human is going towards which horse. She will prick her ears and look at the person who is watching her from a distance and will imperceptibly make the first contact.

If you can manage not to stare at your school horse, but rather gaze into its eyes and really look at it and let it have a peep into your own inner self, then it will begin to communicate with you. It helps to imagine that you're opening a "window to your soul" for the horse and that you are prepared for honest dialogue without misplaced pride and with mutual awareness. Only if you have nothing to hide and can accept the horse with all its idiosyncrasies will you be able to accomplish the in-depth learning process.

We express our emotions through our body language and communicate them to our four-legged partners.

The horse senses our self-confidence and body posture.
With such a supple seat even riding with a neck strap is possible.

From appearance to being

The picture we have of ourselves definitely influences our self-confidence and body language and therefore the way the horse perceives us too. If someone considers him- or herself to be anxious, it will probably show. A decisive change in self-confidence can be initiated by a change in body posture. An upright posture leads to a stronger presence. This is not just visible on the outside,

Anyone who rides with pleasure and sensitivity will be rewarded with an engaged and curious horse.

but is also a mental posture. We straighten up on the inside particularly when we are confident of an exercise, our approach and actions.

With a friendly horse, which is suitable for beginners, and with an experienced instructor, we can test our modified effect on the horse. Take a ball and go into an enclosed space with a loose horse. Don't take any notice of the horse, but concentrate on playing with the ball. There are no rules; you can dribble, throw or kick the ball. All that matters is to do it with concentration and confidence. At the same time resist any thought of involving the animal or making it notice you. Don't try to entice the animal, and don't try to "look good", just concentrate on yourself. Your positive aura and the pleasure you are getting from your physical activity will be transmitted to the horse and communicate fun and safety. You will quickly realize that the less you want from him, the more interested the horse will become in you.

You can build on this by trying to lead the horse without a rope. Walk next to the horse and concentrate utterly on the experience. Most horses will be happy to follow – so long as there are no distractions. Anyone who succeeds in giving the horse freedom of choice will be rewarded with an interested and inquisitive companion.

Please do not blame the horse

Returning riders, just like other riders in fact, have a tendency immediately to blame the horse when something does not go as it is supposed to. Not only is this unfair to another living creature, but it also won't help improve the rider's performance in the slightest. We should avoid taking the horse's supposed wrongdoing personally. It would be better to expect just a little less of the horse and identify our own part in the lesson's failures. Often we don't even notice our own mood swings which we then convey to the horse. Like all people, we are sometimes irritable, distracted or over-ambitious and tend to have unreasonable, emotional reactions. It is equally normal that both our mood and that of our horse are not the same every day. Perhaps the horse could not understand us at all because we gave the aids in an inattentive and inaccurate manner. The horse is not responsible for our moods, our stress or our well-being. Only we ourselves can comprehend our emotions and modify our behaviour accordingly.

What if ...?

Fear

and controlling fear

For many returning riders, fear is an omnipresent theme. Horses and riding have fascinated us since childhood but a myriad of different scenarios, such as the fear of falling, being kicked or bitten, or of a bolting horse, lie deep within us and can stand in the way of our pleasure and lightheartedness. Biologically speaking, fear is meant to protect us from possible harm. Someone who experiences fear is getting a warning from his or her body and can assess situations, discern danger and act accordingly. We should be grateful for our body's protective function and work on our fears instead of getting angry about them or feeling inadequate. For most returning riders, overcoming fear on different levels will be an unavoidable topic.

Don't always imagine the worst

Fears are very intimate feelings. Their emotional meaning and depth vary from one person to another. What one person finds frightening another will see as an exciting challenge. If we feel fear, our brain tries to assess the situation by comparing the frightening incident with memories and similar experiences. If fear increases, it will lead to a series of physical reactions which can also be felt by the horse. These can include increased heart rate, rapid shallow breathing and a significant tensing of the muscles.

Inexperience can make us frightened of horses when we realize that we haven't really come to grips with our planned return to the saddle. It is understandable for anyone who has not correctly assessed his or her attitude to the horse to be afraid. It is the fear of the unknown. If this is the case, then getting more involved with the behaviour of horses in general and getting to know what individual school horses are like will successfully counteract this fear. For example, research has shown that the better educated and enlightened a person is, the less they will be prone to irrational feelings of fear.

Sometimes we feel fear because we have already had bad experiences with horses or in particular situations. Our memory is warning us about getting into a similar situation. Anyone who has fallen off a Haflinger while riding along the beach will perhaps try to avoid Haflingers or riding on the beach or else will take increased safety measures.

Certain fears first appear only after a long break in riding, in particular if we are in doubt about our abilities. Someone who has not had anything to do with horses for a long time will be far more insecure around them than someone who has always been surrounded by horses. This uncertainty can be reinforced if someone warns us about some situation or another and hence conveys a feeling of inadequacy, thus increasing our fears even further.

Quite rightly, returning riders fear physical pain, especially as a result of a fall. Whether from their own experience or from what they know about the horse, everyone knows riding can be a dangerous sport and there is a certain risk involved with being around such large creatures. They can bite, kick, knock us over and we can fall off when riding. This kind of fear is very real and it is quite normal to feel the need to protect yourself from injury.

In order to be able to overcome this type of fear, you should take the need to protect yourself seriously and act accordingly. This means finding out about a horse's possible reactions, observing them carefully in order to anticipate their reactions and training your own capacity to react. It can be helpful to follow appropriate safety precautions when riding such as wearing a riding hat, back protector, sturdy footwear and even wearing gloves when leading a horse in-hand. When fearing a fall, holistic riding instruction is the right way to reactivate your equestrian instincts. It allows you to learn better balance so you feel safer in the saddle regardless of what movement your horse might make. In this way you

Anyone who knows his or her horse well will be better able to understand its behaviour.

Fear of losing control is a strong emotion. Nobody likes to put their fate into the hands of someone else. When riding, our well-being lies to a certain extent in the hooves of the horse and we cannot give the animal any insight into everyday dangers. However much we put our trust in the school horse, the uncertainty still remains as to whether it might get spooked by something, be totally panic stricken, bolt and cause an accident. Objective, targeted exercises, such as relaxation or leadership training, can give us routine and assurance. Step-by-step we will be able to maintain control even in tricky situations.

Other problem areas could be a subliminal fear of commitment, rejection or too much physical intimacy. In such cases horses can represent truly important points of reference since they offer affection without demanding anything in return. With the help of a caring riding instructor and perhaps also a therapeutic coach, valuable insights can be gained from working with the horse and then transferred into everyday life.

Various types of fears of exams are common problems experienced by returning riders. It is important here not to overstretch yourself, but to stick to your aims and the steps to getting there and not to place yourself under undue pressure by competing too soon.

It is always advisable to speak openly to the riding instructor about fear so that they too do not overstretch us during lessons. They often cannot tell what we dare and what we don't dare to do. It doesn't help to ignore fears and thus overstretch ourselves

Modern body protectors don't constrict the rider but protect the back if a fall occurs.

should gradually be in a position to ride out the horse's boisterous little buck during a lesson.

When training on a lead rein, we learn to lead our horse in a safe manner.

and possibly put ourselves at increased risk of accident.

Riders' fears can intensify a horse's discomfort further. This is how a vicious cycle of anxiety can really develop. The worst fears are those we create for ourselves when we paint a picture in minute detail of a doomsday scenario involving all manner of improbable risks of accident. It certainly makes sense to face up to reality and its risks. If we can correctly assess our abilities, we can work out a plan to help work on our shortcomings. These fears should not dominate us but just give us the opportunity to work towards a meaningful solution.

Training for better safety

As a general safety measure when around horses, it is particularly important for returning adult riders to bear in mind what they might have done quite naturally as a child – probably because it was a requirement and not an option. As adults, though, we can decide whether to wear a riding hat or not, but we should be aware that our riding clothes can significantly influence the risks when we are around horses. Although wearing breezy, loose tops may be flattering, it is safer to wear a figure-hugging outfit so we cannot get caught up somewhere or frighten our horse. This is particularly valid for jackets or gilets which should always be done up. This is the only way to stop getting hung up on a branch or fence post for example, when riding past. Modern back protectors no longer impede a rider's movements and it makes particu-

lar sense to wear one when riding across country to protect the rider's upper body from serious injury in case of a fall. Gloves are recommended to protect the hands and sturdy footwear with a heel which will prevent the foot from slipping in the stirrup should be worn as a matter of course.

Sensible behaviour also increases safety when riding and when in contact with horses. For example, never put your finger or your whole hand through eyes or loops in lead ropes or reins in case the horse suddenly pulls at the other end. For the same reason you should never wrap a lead rein around your hand nor attach a lunge rein to your body.

Another important exercise for anyone dealing with horses is to remember when in contact with the horse that it perceives the world around it quite differently from the way we do. For example, a horse cannot see clearly in certain positions. It has blind spots straight in front and behind its head and cannot see anything there unless it turns its head. That is why it makes sense never to approach a horse directly from behind and suddenly touch it, but rather to approach it from the side within its field of vision.

Accidents can also be avoided by not kneeling down or sitting on the ground when close to large animals. A scared horse can accidentally run over a human and there is no way to escape the danger zone quickly from such a position.

Special desensitizing training promotes tranquility in the horse and increases its feeling of trust in humans. If done correctly, the horse will gradually become accus-

When doing specific desensitizing training, you gradually get the horse accustomed to unusual external stimuli.

tomed to different environmental stimuli. New objects or situations will no longer be perceived as a potential danger, but inspected in a playful, curious manner. The person will learn to get to know his or her horse better within a relaxed atmosphere and find out which situations the horse is frightened of and at what distance from a potentially dangerous object it is likely to shy.

Classic desensitizing training exercises involve working with boards and poles, going through difficult passages such as curtains of flapping strips of material or narrow entrances, crossing obstacles such as planks or bridges, overcoming fear of an umbrella opening or a ball being thrown and working on unusual noises such as the hiss of a spray or the rattling of a tractor. The returning rider will thus exert his or her influence and guide the horse through various situations.

Ways of overcoming fear

There is a whole range of different techniques to escape from those insidious attacks of fear. One of them, the visualization technique, forms a part of mental training. Instead of imagining over and over again how an accident could happen, imagine a particular catastrophic scenario and visualize in detail how you would deal with it. Let it appear in your mind's eye as if it were a genuine experience and imagine all the appropriate, safe courses of action and options you have. See how you can behave confidently and turn a risky situation into a great experience from which you can really

grow. You will no longer experience situations which previously filled you with fear and terror as a victim but instead, emerge from these challenges victorious.

Another good way of overcoming your fear is the so-called Anchor Technique. In this method we try to associate a particular emotional state with a trigger. Choose a word which you perceive as positive and think of it every time you find yourself in a stressful situation. Your anchor works its magic within you like a talisman. In a particular moment with the horse when you are feeling really safe, you can choose a buzz word that will symbolize your amazing positive riding skill.

If you believe that your unique sense of balance is the key to harmonious riding, then you could choose the word "balance" as your anchor and repeat it to yourself over and over again during beautiful moments in order to convince your subconscious of the truth of your affirmation. If you then get into a stressful situation with the horse, one that makes you feel insecure, then you will be able to recall your buzz word "balance" which will help make you feel self-confident. It helps diminish inner tension and stops you from getting caught in a panic attack, but rather to approach the situation in a constructive manner.

But have a little patience, it will need to be worked on for a few weeks and months, since a change in perception cannot happen overnight. Your inner anchor, your special word, can also help you in your everyday life away from horses whenever you feel stressed or insecure.

With the help of the so-called "anchor technique", you can learn how to relax and enjoy hacking once more.

Cool down

Because of the way they unfold, journeys within our imagination help us reach a state of relaxation where we can reflect on the essentials of the human–horse relationship. Our imagination knows no boundaries, we can dream of a perfect world. We can infuse our equestrian challenges with limitless positive feelings, far from doubt and lack of assurance. In our imagination we are always a strong partner for our horse. We are beautiful, brave, and heroic – in fact everything our mind wishes to imagine.

With guidance, relaxation exercises and meditation can be a great help to finding inner calm. You can also choose various motivating tunes and songs that embody the kind of relationships you would like to achieve, or whose dynamics encourage you to greater activity or more gentleness. If you let this inner "movie score", which represents various emotions, capture you and listen carefully to it, then you will soon be able to access its associated feelings in stressful situations by imagining your song and acting out the emotions conveyed. In this way you can conquer tricky situations with a powerful orchestra and approach your horse in the grooming area with the sound of harps in your head.

To promote inner peace, it helps to recognize your different internal voices so that you can gradually change them. Who exactly is it that keeps talking to you and what is the voice trying to tell you? Is it the eternal cynic who keeps trying to get you out of an idea by saying things such as "You'll never manage that", or "That won't help any-

thing" and is forever pointing out your weaknesses and failures instead of seeing your successes? Or perhaps it's your favorite enemy who begrudges your success, and belittles you by saying things like "It wasn't really that great", or "Don't flatter yourself"?

Some of these voices are expressions of your inner dissatisfaction and insecurity. You can face up to your niggling self-doubts if at long last you start to see yourself in an exaggeratedly positive manner: "I was the best one of all in that last riding lesson", or "My horse really understands me and would follow me anywhere". Such overstatements don't just strengthen your own self-confidence, they also give you strength for future endeavours.

On the other hand, our heads are often full of negative things other people, such as bad tempered riding instructors or envious riders, have said or derogatory remarks made by our work colleagues. In order not to take them quite so seriously or silence them totally, you can imagine that they sound like a slow-playing tape or the high-pitched voice of someone who has inhaled helium. The less we take what has been said seriously, or to be true, the less we will be influenced by these negative voices which rob us of our positive energy.

You can only be a strong partner for your horse when you are well-adjusted and at peace with yourself.

A miracle of movement on four hooves –

Anatomy and

psyche

of the horse

Only if you engage thoroughly with horses as living creatures will you do them justice and judge precisely what is expected of you after your return to the world of horses. A preference for a particular riding style will soon develop from your own ideal image of riding and this will in turn influence the type of horse that best suits you. Of course you can go over small jumps on a Shire horse, but anyone wanting to do show jumping would be better off on a Warmblood. You are not doing yourself or the horse any favours by trying to learn a discipline which is not within the animal's physical capacity. A moral dilemma emerges in some returning riders: perhaps you would like to learn Baroque riding, but on the other hand you feel a lot safer on a pony than on a big Friesian. Luckily there are compromises: perhaps let go of that dream of a "dressage career" and instead go for a beautiful riding style at a hobby level without exaggerated demands.

Horses –
a masterpiece of nature

As children we probably didn't give much thought to the physique, functional anatomy or state of health of riding school horses. Today as adults we are totally discerning and want to know that our horses are really happy with us and our equestrian intentions.

Learning to ride in a way that protects the back is top priority for the health of both horse and rider.

The horse's back is of vital importance. This after all is where we sit in the saddle and the exact point where the horse bears our weight. Let us take a look at the horse's skeleton and its structure. The spine hangs like a bridge between fore and hind legs. The individual vertebrae allow the horse to flex laterally whilst simultaneously ensuring great stability and flexibility. The horse's back is particularly resilient when several factors are combined. Through appropriate schooling exercises the horse's spine should be properly embedded in the strands of muscles surrounding it. The back should not appear to be sensitive when grooming or touching it. White hairs on a coloured horse's withers usually indicate a healed pressure point from a previously ill-fitting saddle. Deep depressions in the muscles on either side of the withers indicate an unsuitable saddle in conjunction with a style of riding with little respect for the horse's back.

So as not to strain the horse's back excessively, the rider should ride a horse which is appropriate for his or her weight. As a guideline, a horse should not carry more than one-seventh of its body weight. The instructor should be careful to teach their pupils horse-friendly riding in order to protect the horse's back. This includes an elastic seat as well as riding the horse on the bit so that its back can arch. When ridden in a correct outline, the horse's head is stretched forwards and downwards and the back is also rounded. Lacking this, the spine's bridge-like construction will sag and the rider will become an extremely heavy burden for the horse.

Using a mounting block to mount the horse will protect the horse's back since the saddle won't be pulled so strongly to one side by the rider's weight. Using a mounting block shows the rider's caring attitude towards the horse and there is no reason to let your pride stop you from using one.

It is also interesting to note that horses, just like humans, have a preference for one side or the other. They show a so-called natural asymmetry. That is to say they usually find exercises going in one direction easier than the other. It can happen that a school horse would rather gallop or bend to the right. One side is therefore more flexible than the other. Meaningful equestrian training should aim to work on both sides so that no signs of unilateral wear should occur.

A returning rider will strongly feel his or her own right- or left-handedness after a lengthy break from riding. So as to become more flexible and improve coordination it can be useful to carry out routine movements the other way round. You could mount from the right or lead the horse from the right-hand side in order to gain more control over your movements. By doing this you also contribute to a reduction in the horse's one-sided stress.

What is horse-friendly riding?

Horse-friendly riding also means rider-friendly riding. It is kinder on the back because it allows the rider to sit more comfortably and is in line with the performance curve of both horse and rider.

But how do you recognize a riding school which has made horse-friendly riding a core value? In such a place you won't see a horse constrained with tight training aids or which is held so tight it holds its head on its chest. A horse that has such a rolled-up posture cannot round its back correctly. It will always let its back sag and become strained.

Furthermore one can recognize horse-friendly riding where high priority is given to the rider's

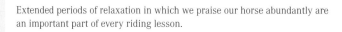
Extended periods of relaxation in which we praise our horse abundantly are
an important part of every riding lesson.

posture and seat. Only a fastidious rider who learns how to find his or her own centre of gravity will be able to balance it over the horse's and thus evolve from being a heavy weight to an elastic rider. Exercises to improve the rider's seat are not harassment from the riding instructor, but are, on the contrary, hugely important for the health of both the school horse and the rider.

A riding instructor who bears the health of horse and human in mind will ensure that both will be encouraged but not overstretched. It is a very bad sign if the horse is covered in sweat and breathless after a riding lesson. No riding lesson should over-tax an animal like this.

A warm-up phase at the beginning of the lesson, as well as a relaxation phase at the end, is extremely important for both horse and rider in order to avoid injuries and pulled muscles. A warm-up run with the horse on a lead rein, jumping over a cavaletti with the horse in-hand or a few stretching exercises in the yard can help our bodies prepare for the riding lesson.

As a form of relaxation after riding, I would recommend a walk with the horses or a relaxing massage or grooming session for your horse. Frequent short pauses should be included during a lesson, in particular for returning riders who are out of practice. It is also advisable for returning riders to work on their own fitness. Aerobic exercise such as jogging or swimming plus some gymnastics will improve the rider's physical fitness. Even people of an advanced age and average fitness can ride. But the fitter and more agile a person, the easier it will be to learn to ride. A good sense of balance also lessens the likelihood of a fall and the risk of injury.

If you've done everything right and your horse feels thoroughly at ease, then it will display its famous "proboscis".

And how does the school horse feel about the riding lesson?

The ABC of body language encompasses the interaction of individual elements of expressive behaviour. These include in particular the horse's facial expression, its muscle tone, heart rate, breathing, vocal expression and whole body posture which you can interpret by "scanning" the individual parts of the body, collating them into a complete picture and analysing it.

Alert horses take an active interest in their surroundings, they look interested, are people-friendly and are motivated to work with humans. They exhibit the typical signs of a happy horse: shining eyes, soft gaze, mobile ears, relaxed muscle tone, elastic movements. Depending on the situ-

Anyone who observes a horse carefully and enters into its world can tell how well it is feeling from its appearance.

ation, the horse can have a playful or a relaxed face. All these behavioural traits can be seen in nature in apparently positive situations such as at play, during mutual grooming or peaceful grazing. They are also signs of the horse's well-being when in contact with humans and when being ridden. Often the horse extends its upper lip into a "proboscis" to express its contentment.

In contrast, agitation will lead to increased muscle tension, a tail held high, prancing, twitching ears and possibly sweating and frequent defecation.

Tense muscles, a head held high, a tail pressed close to the body or jammed between the hind legs, a tense mouth, tense ears laid back flat, flaring nostrils and rolling eyes can be signs of stress and fear in a horse. If you notice heavy sweating, blowing or loud neighing, frequent defecation and increased heart and breathing rates, then it is likely that the horse's stress level has increased significantly. Each horse has a very different way of showing stress. There are introverts and extroverts who exhibit outward signs to varying degrees. Accurate observation and understanding of the horse's psyche are required.

The number one objective of any training should be the horse's positive expression. In my opinion there is no point in practising a lesson unless the horse is happy to cooperate. If it is not, it will never have that shine and expressiveness we seek. Riding means a union. If that togetherness is absent, then you will never achieve synchronization in movement and true harmony. The foundation for such intimacy is trust and inner contentment.

Recognizing when the horse is in pain

Since riding pupils shouldn't allow school horses to suffer, you should learn as soon as possible to recognize symptoms of illness or injury. Being able to recognize the first signs of pain can be extremely important.

Anxiety can affect both humans and horses as a kind of warning signal from the body to define actual or perceived unpleasant external influences on the body. Nature has made it possible for the horse, as well as for other creatures, to discern things which are dangerous for the body and to protect themselves instinctively from further pain. You have to differentiate between acute painful reactions which are of short duration and are a direct response to a specific, painful situation, and chronic pain which can last months or years and have more than one cause.

In the case of acute pain and depending on the different type of effect it has on the body (for example an injury or inflammation), the body perceives the stimulus through pain receptors. These are transmitted via the nerves to the brain which then leads to complex, very individual and strong sensations. Chronic pain however is hard to identify and treat as sufferers learn to live with their handicap and the pain increasingly takes on a life of its own which makes it impossible to trace it back to one particular cause.

The way pain is felt and its manifestations are as varied in horses as in humans and are very different for each organism. The range of expression of pain is equally broad. Some horses suffer quite clearly, their faces speak volumes even for small injuries. Others are much tougher and hide their feelings of pain. In general though, for all animals, facial expressions change when they are in pain. Their eyes glaze over, their expression is empty or internalized, their ears are often pressed against the skull or hang loosely and face diagonally to the rear. The face muscles tighten so that the larger

blood vessels become more visible below the skin and the lips become tight, showing wrinkles. The nostrils are stretched or flared through strained breathing. It is particularly difficult to identify pained faces in sturdy breeds when they have their winter coats since the characteristic muscle changes are hidden by their long coats.

A horse's whole expression can change radically, in particular in the case of chronic pain. Often the only evidence of pain will be the expression in its eyes. Such horses appear apathetic and expressionless.

Pain often influences the horse's whole behaviour. In addition to characteristic reactions to certain types of pain, for example limping following a leg injury, the horse's body reacts with stress symptoms. Depending on the degree of pain, the horse will breathe faster and more shallowly, sweat even though it is apparently calm, and its blood pressure and sometimes temperature will rise. Many horses avoid unnecessary movement when in pain. However there are extrovert types of horses that become restless and try to "run away" from the pain.

It is important that returning riders get to know the various school horses and their individual facial or other expressions when they are in a normal, healthy state. You could note their vital signs (pulse, respiration and temperature) so that in case of doubt you could calculate variations from the norm and determine how great the differences are. You could also ask the riding instructor to include a theory lesson on horse health. Riding pupils could learn how to measure the most important vital signs such as pulse, breathing and temperature

and how to assess the measurements. At rest, large prominent blood vessels are visible on some horses' heads whilst with others you can hardly see any at all. You can only come to a conclusion about the actual state of a particular animal when you compare it to its "average facial expression". This is the same as the way we learn to appreciate signs of malaise in our friends' faces and posture.

We can see how well this horse is feeling just by looking at his facial expression.

Horse-friendly contact

Our contact with horses is always appropriate to the animal if we are predictable in our dealings with it and treat it in a fair, loving manner. This means that we should first think about our own targets and desires in order to follow up on them when riding or caring for the horse. Positive reinforcement - reward training - is, for example, a motivating form of training and contact. Horses find learning easy and are happy to engage in it when they don't feel fear and can learn while being free from pressure and threat of punishment. If we want positive contact with the horse, it is important to break away from any ubiquitous riding traditions and seek positive learning alternatives. Clicker training is a nonviolent training method based on positive reinforcement.

Loving care from a human is very important to the horse. Horses should enjoy being touched. Some horses prefer to be stroked gently, others prefer energetic scratching or full body massages. Finding favourite scratching spots and giving the horse enjoyable body contact will influence both the horse's and human's feelings of happiness.

When being ridden, a horse is always happy if it has learned an exercise through positive reinforcement and has been neither over- nor under-stretched. In my opinion, variety plays a large part. As far as I'm concerned, the most important issue for creating a happy relationship between human and horse is the attitude of the human. Only someone who is truly attracted

emotionally to his or her horse and accepts its uniqueness will be able to transmit that attraction. The horse's happiness also depends on whether we manage to love

Go exploring and discover where your horse likes to be scratched best.

our horse unreservedly with all its strengths and weaknesses. Just like us humans, a horse needs to feel appreciated and not just measured by its performance or beauty. The happiness of both human and horse will result when the human has no egotistical expectations of the horse but is only interested in true togetherness.

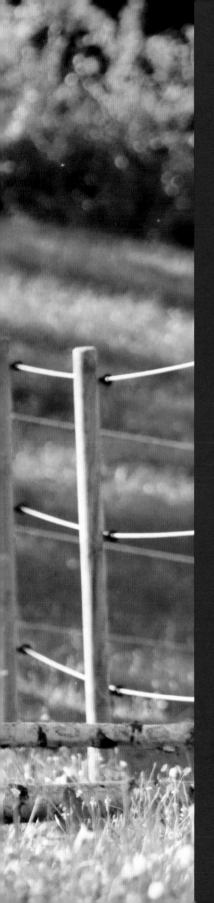

Balance
with feeling –
Learning the movements

It is said that you never forget how to ride, just like you never forget how to swim or ride a bike. Depending on how well you used to ride, with a little patience you will sooner or later be able to bring those submerged skills back to the surface. Your body has stored up those typical equestrian movement patterns deep within your muscle memory. At first your muscles will ache and you will be surprised by how stiff you have become over the years. In general that feeling for the horse's movements comes back quickly. Everyone has a distinct sense of their own body and former riders have already trained their muscle memory for the long term when riding in their youth.

Off the couch and into the saddle

Returning riders know their weak inner-self well, the one who would like to stop them from leaving their comfort zone. It's just so much cosier on the couch... . An individual's comfort zone can be defined as the area in which they feel good and safe. Anything strenuous can make us feel afraid or unsafe and will trigger our weak inner-self which will think of endless reasons why we would rather spend our free time with it on the couch.

Usually you can only manage the leap from non-rider to rider with a bit of diligence

Get off your sofa and get out into the natural environment with your horse!

A brisk ride out in the fields stimulates all our senses.

and a courageous stride out of your comfort zone. This is where you will be able to exceed yourself and be proud of your achievements. It can be helpful to convince yourself simply to step into the zone of uncertainty just once and delight in small attainable achievements.

Your subconscious can once again help you on your way to broadening your sphere of achievement. If you work on your own self-image and develop more confidence, then your subconscious will accept that you can achieve much more. You can "programme" your subconsciousness with so-called neuro-associative conditioning. This kind of programming usually functions in three successive phases.

During the first phase you become aware of why you really should urgently change something, become braver or look for a riding school for returning riders. What is the motivation for this? Of course there are arguments which are obviously in favour of becoming braver, such as, for example, being able to enjoy a gallop over a field of stubble and thus experience a long-held dream of riding. On the other hand, your life in the comfort zone is very predictable and you may be afraid of the unknown. However, if you left things as they are, you would probably be left with negative feelings. It could be that other riders have managed it and you cannot keep putting it off for ever. Don't get me wrong, nobody is obliged to gallop when out on a ride if they don't want to. We are just talking about a common example of a returning rider's typical dream.

Phase one will be complete when you have discovered the psychological leverage effect for yourself as well as the supporting motivation required to let you make the change. The fact that you cannot be satisfied with the status quo should silence that weak inner-self. The joy at the prospect of change should prevail. In the subsequent phase, you will decisively interrupt your familiar behaviour pattern if you run the risk of repeating it. When you are just about to answer your riding instructor that you do not have time to go out on a ride on Sunday, you should say to yourself, "Stop, that is not what I want at all". This is how to interrupt your habitual train of thought. It will become even clearer for your subconscious if, at the same time, you behave in an out of the ordinary way and suddenly jump up and down with apparent joy and answer "Yes, I'd love that". It is of course important to choose an activity that seems perfectly achievable to you - to go for a quiet walk on a lead rein rather than that gallop over fields of stubble

of your dreams. The most important thing is to step out on your way to making a change.

The third phase of neuroassociative conditioning is the reinforcement phase. This is where you seek to combine your new behaviour patterns with enjoyment. You imagine how it will be when you have reached your objective and give yourself abundant praise for the partial progress you have made. You can by all means reward yourself for your bravery and perseverance, for example with a meal out or by buying yourself a treat from the riding shop. It is not just the horse, but also the human who learns best when motivated by small rewards.

An active seat – letting yourself move

To achieve a dynamic, active seat which follows the horse's movements, you will need to concentrate on your own inner movements stimulated by those of the horse. The horse moves your body quite naturally in each of the various gaits according to different specific movement patterns. A good way to improve your seat is to imagine that you really are being moved by the horse and that you are really experiencing this movement in all its dimensions.

We can feel the horse's power, dynamics and rhythm and the up and down movements of its back as well as its breathing and hear the sound of its hooves, feel the wind in our hair and smell that typical horse smell. This complete picture will help you to be as one with the animal's

Why not sit back-to-front on the horse and enjoy a truly different view?

movements. If in addition to all this you can think of a good reason why, for example, you want to experience that gallop which you so loved as a child once more, then you will have the beginnings of further improvement to your riding style.

If, while riding, you are able to get in touch with your deeper physical sensations, then you will be able to use these experiences to practise without a horse in between lessons. Here you could learn consciously to explore each part of your body, feel each movement and experience your various muscles in all their strength. Later on you can bring those physical sensations into harmony with the feelings of movement on horseback.

If we feel deep down inside our bodies, we can visualize the groups of muscles we use for different movements like going up stairs or riding a bicycle. If, when doing these everyday movements, you are in tune with your physical activity, then you can imagine the internal movements involved in riding and relate to them so you can get a feeling for harmony. It is extremely abstract to read about how the aids for canter should look, where each leg should be positioned and how your hands should be held. It is much simpler to refer to your muscle memory and imagine how that canter stride felt. The aids for canter include an intuitive seat at each stride. The horse places us in that position because we allow it to and we have developed sufficient balance and stability.

Little by little, set yourself increasingly complex movement pattern exercises when doing your dry training. How exactly would it feel riding a horse cantering on the left rein and jumping cavaletti? The nerve pathways needed for our inner riding are exactly the same as those for real riding. The same technique can be observed in endurance sportsmen, skiers or bobsleigh drivers for example, who go through the course in their heads before a competition. In this way, you are training your movements in your imagination exactly as you will do them later on, on the horse. Perhaps you can remember movement highlights from your childhood. What was it like standing on a cantering horse? Or perhaps sitting back to front on the horse's back? These unusual movement patterns increase the body's skill incredibly. If you have never sat backwards on a horse, you should really try it out under supervision. It is a truly novel experience and gives a totally different viewpoint.

Searching for your centre of gravity

Finding the centre of your body, your own centre of gravity, is pivotal for reliving those old, somewhat rusty movement channels when looking to rediscover positive physical sensations. Anyone who is really good at finding his or her own centre of gravity, and can get this as close as possible to the horse's, will manage to find a seat with ideal posture and excellent balance. It can be helpful consciously to practise different movements when trying to find your own centre of gravity. How about standing as still as possible on one leg? Once you have

Touching your toes teaches you balance.

Stretching your arms in the air facilitates riding without reins and improves balance.

got that feeling, you can make the exercise a bit more difficult by stretching that leg out rather than just keeping it close to your body. Trying to stand still like that requires balance and muscle tone. Anyone who cannot stand straight will find it difficult to keep this balance.

Think of a ballet dancer. To execute difficult pirouettes, her body is stretched to the maximum but is not tense. She knows precisely at which point to turn her body so as not to fall. Your own centre of grav-

ity lies protected beneath your navel in the pelvic area. A helpful image to illustrate this, is to imagine a glass ball moving back and forth in a bowl as the horse rolls our "ball" around in our pelvis. The horse's centre of gravity lies conveniently below the rider, deep within its thorax. When riding in harmony, your own centre of gravity will always lie above that of the horse. By consciously shifting your centre of gravity you also cause the horse's balance to shift. This is an important basis for giving precise aids and in particular for developing lateral schooling movements when riding.

You can also gain suppleness in your movements by practising them on the horse, for example touching your toes in the stirrups and bending right down, stretching your arms out or putting them round the horse's neck. All of this is to be done under supervision.

Learning to feel

During training, the first thing to learn is the notion of rhythm. It can be defined as a spatial and temporal regularity at each of the horse's gaits and should be maintained on straight lines, curves or during a change of pace. Walk has a four-stroke rhythm; trot has a two-stroke rhythm and canter three-stroke. You can practise your

Feeling for the right moment to urge the horse on can be developed particularly well when riding bareback.

feeling for the strokes of the different gaits by counting out loud when on the horse's back, just as in a dancing lesson.

Riding with your eyes shut while someone leads the horse can also be enlightening. You can feel the step sequence even more clearly when riding bareback. Our hips do not just move up and down, they also move in a three-dimensional pivoting movement from front to back as well as from left to right. If you can really get inside the feeling of your legs, you will notice that there are moments when one leg is drawn noticeably closer to the horse's belly. These are the precise moments for urging the horse forwards as the horse's belly approaches each leg alternately, swinging back as the horse moves the corresponding hind leg forwards and the belly muscles follow the movement rhythmically. If you want to stimulate the horse to push off energetically then it is only at this particular moment that your leg can influence the rhythm and get the horse to move its hind leg more energetically. It is particularly effective if you say or think "now" to yourself to indicate which hind leg is moving forwards.

Shaking off dissatisfaction

Time and again I come across returning riders who fall into the trap of a negative performance spiral. Of course it is great to improve and encourage yourself onwards. It is however counterproductive to believe: "The more I achieve in a short space of time, the better." Here you are aspiring to gallop today, join the local hunt tomorrow and shine in the piaffe–passage tour at the Baroque horse gala the day after. Such ex-

aggerated aspirations will all too often lead to an impasse, they overstretch riders and give them the feeling that their performance is insufficient, and they will never be satisfied.

I consider this to be a most unsatisfactory state which prevents riders from appreciating even partial successes and enjoying the actual equestrian stage they have reached. We need those performance plateaux in order to take in and enjoy the current level before taking the next step forward.

Sometimes that inner dissatisfaction can also stem from the presumed expectations of our fellow riders. Yet we should listen to our own needs and wishes in the first place, and not try to do right by others. Small successes which may seem insignificant to the outsider can make us feel very happy, for example being greeted affectionately by our horse or when she stands in a well behaved manner whilst giving us her hoof.

Riding in a snow globe

One of the key abilities of good riders is their capacity to concentrate and not to let external factors distract them. This means that when you are riding, you are only riding and not doing anything else. Mistakes can be analysed and discussed during pauses, resolutions made later. Whilst riding, you should be feeling and acting, and nothing else besides. Each annoyance about a messed up lesson or a thought about something to be done later will interfere with the body's intuitive actions.

If you operate at too much of an intellectual level, you will slow down your intuitive

Even when out riding with the family, you must remain totally aware of both yourself and your horse.

feel for riding. Riding has a lot to do with sinking into a world of movement. Just as children get so absorbed in their game of Cowboys and Indians that they forget to go in for lunch, you can imagine that you are riding in your own magic world – in a snow globe. Any disturbing outside influences will bounce off the globe's glass exterior. Everyday worries disappear; they'll be back soon enough. You can decide on the atmosphere and your pace of learning inside your snow globe. You are the guardian of your closed-off world. This picture of a snow globe should enable you to construct a safe shelter for yourself and to have the right, for once, to escape from your stressful everyday life.

The
scale
of progression for training the rider –

Learning how to give the aids

One thing that is certain, is that returning riders cannot expect all their previously acquired knowledge and ability suddenly to bloom again from one moment to the next. Many things only come back with time and practice, when the necessary muscle strength has been built back up and insecurities swept away. Only once this stage has been reached can you start to rediscover individual core themes and concern yourself with refining the aids in order to achieve more harmony with the horse and set the stage to live out your own dreams, whether this be to try to compete in one of the disciplines, go on a trek or to think eventually about buying your own horse.

There's no such thing as a correct seat

An important point to realize is that there is no one, unique, correct riding seat. Each riding style has its own seat which, depending on the discipline, is far removed from the seat adopted in the other various disciplines. A keen show jumper will need a so-called light seat with relatively short stirrup leathers. They shift their body weight onto their knee joints and stirrups, their upper body bends forwards from the hips and their hands lie at the base of the mane towards the horse's mouth so that the horse can stretch over the jump.

The dressage rider, on the other hand, has a classic dressage seat where they sit straight and deep in the saddle with their knees and upper thighs flush to the saddle. When looked at from the side, the shoulder, hip and heel should lie in a vertical line.

You will naturally sit quite differently on a different saddle, for example a Western saddle with a centre of gravity that is situated further back than a dressage saddle. Each and every type of seat however is crucial for the health of the horse. Whatever the riding style, the rider must sit in as balanced a way as possible without putting extra weight on one side of the horse.

The returning rider should also consider the fact that no two people are anatomically identical and that each one will have to develop his or her own seat.

Someone who has short thighs compared with the length of their lower leg will sit in a different way and will find their centre of gravity in a different way from someone whose thigh to lower leg ratio is exactly the opposite. Each body shape has its own challenge. Since the pelvises of men and women are differently shaped, a woman's seat will be different from that of a man. The returning rider will only be able to make progress in his or her ability and learn more about his or her own seat if the riding instructor is aware of these anatomical differences rather than relying on the usual empty phrases such as "hands low" or "shoulders back".

The correct riding seat depends on the individual's physique and riding style.

Sit up straight please!

To find your own straight seat, you can try out a little exercise. Mount a saddled horse that someone is holding and put your upper legs over the front of the saddle. Now move your pelvis forward as deep as you can in the saddle's centre of gravity without hitting your pubic bone on the pommel. Now put your legs back in the riding position by pivoting first one leg then the other from the hips outwards and backwards till you feel them hanging down heavily. Put your feet back in the stirrups, then if you slowly bend right forward and then right back you will get the feeling of a straight body. After repeating that exercise several times you will find a point somewhere in the middle where your back is vertical. This exercise is particularly effective if done with your eyes shut whilst imagining where you would fall if the horse weren't there any more. Would you fall on your behind, which is what should happen if you have a perfect seat, or on your feet?

Another exercise for getting a straight back is to roll your upper body forwards with your chin on your chest and with as round a back as possible. When straightening up it is helpful to imagine that you are building up your spine, vertebra by vertebra. The lumbar vertebrae are the foundation of

a straight back; the chest and neck vertebrae help to balance your heavy head. If the lower part of your spine is crooked, you will not be able to sit up straight and supple.

Putting your thighs forward over the saddle flaps will allow you to find the deepest point of the saddle.

Everything simultaneously

A particular difficulty when learning to ride again is the fact that you often have to give several aids simultaneously. Coordinating the aids can be a real challenge when the manner of holding the reins has to be adapted to the shifting of

Riding is a complex process, which is best learnt subconsciously.

your own centre of gravity and the position of the leg. It requires a good level of body awareness and coordination to succeed. As there is such a multitude of components to perform at the same

time, the list of things to watch out for will be practically endless. Nobody can consciously and simultaneously think about lowering their heel a little more, while lifting their head up, having a straight back and then setting the horse's pace and direction. It is also far too much to expect for a rider to take such statements as "a tenth of a second after going into canter, you should move your inner hip forwards" seriously. It is simply impossible to take stock of, learn or refine, such a complex process as riding in one go and in all its complexities.

A good riding instructor will single out important parts of any particular exercise and concentrate on them for a while. If you happen to be working on holding the reins, you should simply focus on this and separate out the various hand grips in detail. In this way you can imagine closing your fist as if you were holding a small bird in your hand as well as the reins. You hold it tight enough so it doesn't fly away, but gently enough so that you don't harm its fragile body. This image is far more meaningful than if the riding instructor were to say "you can press your fourth finger another half a centimetre onto the palm of your hand". Images should be meaningful to you and if possible appeal to your emotions. They should make a physical action clearer so that you can empathize with the image and act accordingly.

A good riding instructor will give positive feedback when a rider improves his or her seat or does something correctly. Only if you get confirmation of a correct action at that precise moment will the body be able to store the associated physical sensation.

A horse trotting with good rhythm and impulsion is a sheer pleasure for the rider.

From rhythm to elasticity

Not only are there particular points that are important for a rider's training, such as balance, coordination of the aids or concentration whilst on horseback, but there are also guidelines in respect of the horse which the rider absolutely has to learn. In other words, you can only establish horse-friendly riding when you ensure that all your aids reach the horse in a direct and precise manner so the horse fully understands them and so the actions can then be carried out correctly. The six points on the training scale are rhythm, elasticity, contact with the bit, impulsion, rectitude and collection. To a certain extent the individual points represent increasing levels of difficulty, but in many respects they condition one another and can therefore often only be worked on together.

Rhythm, which is the spatial and temporal measure of all the gaits, is the basis of good riding. It will only make sense to go on to more difficult lessons once the returning rider has learned to keep the horse regular in its movements during turns and transitions. The horse's suppleness is also a building block of riding. A supple horse will move with a swinging back, a neck stretched forwards and with rhythmic, relaxed, unhurried movements. It reacts without tension to the rider's aids.

Contact with the bit can only happen with a horse that is not being held tightly with the reins, but rather when the rider stimulates a flow of movement from the hind legs over the horse's back via the rider's body through the reins to the horse's head and without blocking the horse. This requires a high level of sensitivity to the horse's movements. Only when ridden like this can a horse develop impulsion, which is the impulse for movement originating from the hindquarters, the horse's engine.

It is also important to keep the horse straight, to exercise it so that it is equally at ease on both sides of its body and so that the rear hooves step into the traces of the corresponding front hooves. This is a prerequisite for being able to execute a lesson correctly on both reins. The highest objective on the training scale, at an advanced stage, would be the collection of the horse. A collected horse engages its hindquarters under its body, strongly arches its back and is thus able to carry out difficult dressage moves such as a correct piaffe without causing long-term damage to its health.

You can ride well and correctly at every level. Since training and schooling can take many years, even when working correctly, not every returning rider can aim for supremely collected riding. It really is not essential for healthy riding. You should not let yourself be tempted to ride exercises in an incorrect manner just for show if the basics for doing so have not yet been achieved. Thorough foundation work is worthwhile and will later allow you to progress successfully and faster if you have the time and the inclination to do so.

Recognizing suppleness

A supple horse radiates tranquillity in its flowing, diligent movements, while its tail sways loosely from side to side to the rhythm of its paces. Its back swings lightly back and forth and its facial expression shows its contentment. In particular, a relaxed jaw and a loose lower neck muscle are the signs of a horse's suppleness. The rider will notice it because it is easier to sit to the horse's movements and the sound of its hooves hitting the ground is quite quiet.

In contrast, a horse which is tense has little rhythm, but has rather short, clipped movements, a clearly defined lower neck muscle and an unhappy expression on its face. The horse tucks its tail away, presses it between its hindquarters, carries it rigid and crooked to one side or whips it from side to side. Particular discontent when being ridden is shown by tension in the area of the mouth, grinding teeth, excess sweating, loud breathing without noticeable physical exertion and grunting.

You can recognize a supple horse by its relaxed facial expression as well as the engagement of its hind legs beneath its body.

When riding in a pair, each rider focuses more on the choreography and the coordination with his or her partner and therefore rides in a more intuitive manner.

Learning to ride intellectually

Every rider learns to discover and utilize hidden potential at his or her own rhythm. Getting back in the saddle will be particularly easy if you can organize your learning intellectually, that is to say, to network both subconscious and conscious learning content. Only a combination of these learning facets will lead to a concrete result.

Anyone who spends too much time repeating facts and theoretical instructions will not have sufficient time for playful experimentation to develop their own skills. In general when it comes to understanding, humans are best able to retain facts, however where riding is concerned, this essentially needs to be learned and practised at a subconscious level.

Nobody would ever dream of giving a child lengthy explanations of how to ride a bike, how to find their balance. Instead you briefly explain that you put your feet on the pedals, your bottom on the saddle and your hands on the handlebars and then you give the child a little help to find their balance. This is how we all learned to ride a bike when we were children, trusting in our natural sense of balance. This can be done with children also when it comes to riding. They learn intuitively and are streets ahead of returning riders, since as adults we always try to achieve a rational level of understanding.

So that we don't neglect the all-important subconscious learning process, it is useful to get as close as possible to a child-like approach to riding and certainly include playful elements. For example, when on an orienteering ride in the woods, our intellectual focus will be on reading the map and solving the problem we've been set, while our body automatically gets into the horse's movement without conscious thought. The same is achieved riding a *pas de deux* to music. Rousing music stimulates our sense of hearing and our intellect is busy learning the choreography while our subconscious can get in tune with the rhythm. It is particularly helpful if the music has the same rhythm as that of the animal and the style of music supports the subconscious learning task, for example a dynamic piece of music will stimulate a rather slack rider to become more energetic and stable.

Even within these interconnections, you can always choose those elements that awaken your playful nature, that fit your character and trigger positive emotions. Some might prefer feeling like a cowboy with Western riding, camp fires and country music, while others might prefer to imagine themselves as dancing to classical music with their partner, the horse. Your subconscious will only try to achieve your ideal if the image is really harmonious.

Good riding instruction will tie the two learning levels together by imparting knowledgeable explanations about each lesson as well as using games, appealing music, pictorial comparisons and visualization exercises.

The rider's soft gaze

Our emotional awareness is totally different depending on whether we stare fixedly at something, or whether, as when riding a bike, we just let the landscape roll gently by. Your body posture changes automatically when you look at something fixedly. For example, you lean slightly towards the object, hold your breath in a little or tense your muscles. In contrast we don't focus on anything in particular when we have a soft gaze, but just let our surroundings as a whole affect us. We remain more relaxed and enjoy the experience more intensely with this sort of gaze. When riding, you shouldn't desperately look for points in the arena and focus on them, but rather let the whole environment exert its effect on you. You can also add a relaxed smile to that soft, far-reaching look. If you concentrate too much you often clench your jaws together and thus tense your jaw and nape of the neck. If you smile, you get into a positive mood and can tackle problems in a more casual, relaxed way.

With a tender expression in our eyes, we let the world drift by.

Epilogue:

Your own way to the horse

All returning riders have one thing in common however different their path might be: the desire to find happiness on earth on the back of a horse. To a certain extent this is perhaps man's oldest dream – literally to be able to fly freely. You can feel this freedom with a horse. It helps us have more mobility and speed. It takes us on a journey through the most diverse movements.

To truly enjoy this feeling of happiness when riding, you really have to manage to make it an integral part of your daily life and become completely absorbed in it – a state known in psychology as the state of flow. We become a part of the flow of time, there is a moment of complete harmony, and we feel ourselves neither overwhelmed nor unchallenged, but just experience the present with happiness. From a physical aspect this condition is also very special. Heartbeat, blood pressure and breathing are optimally synchronized. We experience a feeling of elation and euphoria. Important prerequisites for experiencing this state are, on the one hand, working towards our objective, but on the other hand not just focusing on it, but on the actions that surround it. Our perception of time will alter: action and consciousness will blend into a state of joy. In this state you will experience the often quoted "lightness of being" and forget your everyday worries.

Of course you cannot rekindle the sunny lightheartedness of your childhood since the world has moved on and you along with it. But now, as an adult lover of horses, you have the necessary maturity to experience this wonderful hobby in your own way. You now know what you like and what is good for you, but you can also precisely express what disturbs your emotional balance and which experiences with horses you are no longer prepared to tolerate. I hope that after reading this book, you, as a returning rider, will have become aware of the fantastic opportunities, but also the ubiquitous stress factors of this hobby. Give yourself time, think about your needs and listen to your intuition so that this new chapter in your life can lead you to sheer happiness.

And finally the most important aspect of getting back in the saddle: the well-being of our beloved horses. These wonderful animals didn't ask for our self-fulfilment to take place on their backs. On the contrary, the well-being of the horse should always take pride of place. Horses need a natural living environment with other horses and not solitary confinement. Even here, through his or her choice, the returning rider decides which type of living conditions he or she supports. Also horse training should not be based on pressure and punishment since nowadays we know that learning through positive reinforcement is far more effective, and above all a more appropriate alternative.

Do not hesitate to make a new start together with that gentle four-legged friend in the way that you want. Do not hesitate for once to step away from the well-trodden path of all the usual equestrian traditions.

I wish you much joy and every success!

Appendix

Thanks

I would particularly like to thank
Conny for her wonderful photos as
well as all my two- and four-legged
models for their time and enthusiasm.

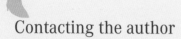

Contacting the author

www.pferdsein.de

Marlitt Wendt's website with
information about looking after horses
and creative horse training as well as
seminar and lecture offers.

Index

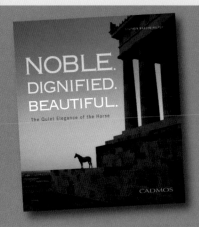

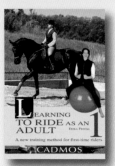
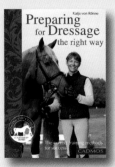